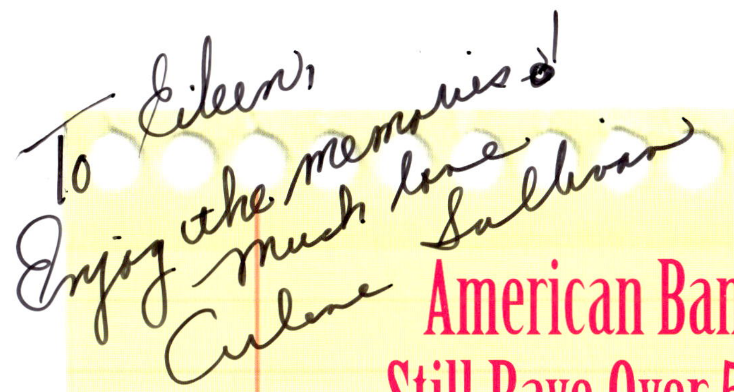

American Bandstand Fans Still Rave Over 50 Years Later!

"I wish kids today had something like American Bandstand. *Great memories."*

—Judie Hupcey

"In the 1950s my best girlfriend, Peggy, and I would hurry to my house from Chesterton High School, where, after having an after-school snack of my mother's homemade cookies or gingerbread, we would dance to the songs on American Bandstand. *We danced in front of the television and when the winners of the dance contest were called to come forward, that would, of course, always be Peggy and Judy. We would walk a few steps closer to the television. Afterward we would laugh and laugh at our pretense of being right there in person and winning."*

—Judy Berrios

"I remember my mom watching Bandstand every day. When I came home from grade school, I would watch it with her! Sometimes we danced together. Mom is 85 now, but still does the jitterbug!"

—Terry DeFelice

"So I watched American Bandstand *from 1961 to 1963. Each day I would run home from the bus stop and flip on the television switch without even removing my coat! I was supposed to be helping with the household chores, but instead had more of an eye on the black-and-white screen. Mom would comment what a poor job of housekeeping I was doing. What great memories of youth!"*

—Sharon Lyons Wardlow

"It took me to a different place with a different group of friends. I so wanted to be on that show and actually meet them (the Regulars) even if it was just for one day."

—Jeff Karlin

"I remember my mom saying if my grades fell then I could not watch American Bandstand *every afternoon, so I ended up getting all As all through high school."*

—Luci Crittenden

"My friend and I were watching one day and were very concerned that Arlene and Kenny were not dancing together. We were so afraid that they had broken up. We decided to send a telegram to the show to find out what happened. We called Western Union and I began telling this operator what to say. When she interrupted me to explain that I had to go to a Western Union Office and pay for the telegram, I just hung up, embarrassed. But this is how much the kids on the show meant to us."

—Sharon Lowery

"I loved watching the dancers and learning the steps to the latest dances, getting to know the Regulars and copying their hairstyles and outfits, the guest stars and Dick Clark during the Philly years."

—Dorothy Meade Miley

"I watched every day after school. We had the best dancers in Philly! I loved to see who was dancing with whom, and learn the latest dance steps. I can't imagine my teen years without Dick Clark and Bandstand*!"*

—Peggy Mcnally

"I couldn't wait to get home from school and tune into American Bandstand*. In fact, when I joined the Marines in 1961, I happened to find a magazine with some Regulars with their fan club addresses. I took a chance and wrote Arlene Sullivan a short letter, telling her that I was a big fan and missed watching the show. To my amazement, a few weeks later I received a letter from Arlene. She thanked me for the kind words and said if I was ever in Philadelphia to look her up. Needless to say, that made my day. Thank you* Bandstand Diaries *for allowing me to share this fond memory."*

—Frank Santangelo

"The introduction into the show panning over the dancers would always bring 'butterflies' in our stomachs. We got to experience the latest in dance moves and more to talk about at school with our friends the next day. Not only did my parents approve of me watching American Bandstand, *my mother would also be just as excited as my girlfriend and I to watch it. It was the greatest show ever. Thank you, Dick Clark, for opening the door to some great teenage years."*

—Donna Frizzell

"There was everything to love about American Bandstand! *Kids like us dancing and romancing. And boy, could they dance! The romances—Arlene and Kenny, Justine and Bob, and how they fit together like pieces of a puzzle! The beautiful Carole Scaldeferri and Frani Giordano! The amazing Pat Molittieri, who danced her heart out everyday! The artists who got their start on* Bandstand *and took over the charts with their hits of the greatest music ever made! Happily so many of them live on to perform and keep the music coming! And last but not least, the irreplaceable Dick Clark, then known as 'America's Oldest Living Teenager!'* American Bandstand *was the reason that teenagers ran home from school every day, so they wouldn't miss a moment of the forever iconic show. Though long gone, Long Live* American Bandstand!*"*

—Jackie West Grasso

"I was on American Bandstand *on the very last day of taping in Philadelphia. It was very emotional for me and everybody else. We weren't happy with Dick because he was moving to Los Angeles. I remember at the very end of the show when they put up the map of the USA. All the Regulars were squeezing in there trying to get on camera for the last time. Afterward, a bunch of us were sitting in the back of the studio watching a play-back tape. Then we put on our coats and left for the very last time."*

—Pat Kinzer Mancuso

Bandstand Diaries
The Philadelphia Years, 1956–1963
Collector's Limited Edition

By Arlene Sullivan, Ray Smith, and Sharon Sultan Cutler

Published November 2016 by Coney Island Press, Inc.
www.bandstanddiaries.com

Publisher's Cataloging-In-Publication Data
(Prepared by The Donohue Group, Inc.)

Names: Sullivan, Arlene, 1942- | Smith, Ray (Ray Joseph), 1942- | Cutler, Sharon Sultan.
Title: Bandstand diaries : the Philadelphia years, 1956-1963 / Arlene Sullivan, Ray Smith, Sharon Sultan Cutler.
Description: First edition. | Collector's limited edition. | Chicago : Coney Island Press, 2016. | Includes index.
Identifiers: ISBN 978-0-9976221-0-2
Subjects: LCSH: American Bandstand (Television program)--History. | Popular music fans--Pennsylvania--Philadelphia--Diaries. | Extras (Actors)--Pennsylvania--Philadelphia--Diaries. | Rock musicians--United States--History.
Classification: LCC PN1992.77.A44 S85 2016 | DDC 791.45/72--dc23

LCCN: 2016946906

20 19 18 17 16 10 9 8 7 6 5 4 3 2 1

Production, design, and print management by Conspire Creative (www.conspirecreative.com).

Contents

Introduction

By Bobby Rydell

To appear on *American Bandstand* was everyone's dream. For the teenagers who were lucky enough to become Regulars, it meant instant popularity, and fun. For a starry-eyed teenage singer like myself who just wanted to perform since childhood, it meant everything.

Little did we know what crowding into that small studio at 46th and Market Streets meant to the rest of America. A sweater worn a certain way, a type of pin on a blouse, a hairstyle (invented the night before) became instant fads across the country because a Regular or performer wore them. The reach of *American Bandstand* to America's teenagers was powerful, and direct. And, for a performer, if the Regulars liked your songs in the Record Review segment, you were golden.

Young Bobby Rydell.

I would hang around the *American Bandstand* studios just trying to get a break. My big day finally came in 1959. Dick Clark had listened to several of my demos and nixed all of them, until he heard *Kissin' Time*. He pronounced it a hit on the spot! The following week, I performed it on the show; the rest, as they say, is history. Dick was completely in touch with what kids liked. His intuition for spotting and predicting a future hit was a gift and rare.

In 1960 with *Kissin' Time*, I joined Dick Clark's *Caravan of Stars* on its summer tour across the United States. I was the youngest person on that tour. I followed *Kissin' Time* with *We Got Love*, *Wild One*, *Volare*, and *Sway*. Every one of my gold records debuted on *American Bandstand*; and because of the exposure I received on the show I am listed in *Billboard Magazine* in the Top 5 recording artists of my era.

If Dick invited a new performer to appear on *American Bandstand*, his or her career took off. I owe my career to Dick Clark; so do many other artists, including my good friends Frankie Avalon and Fabian. I still perform frequently with them as The Golden Boys.

I knew many of the Regulars. I still keep in touch with many of them today, including my great buddy Frank Spagnuola whom I've known for over 70 years, and the one-and-only Arlene Sullivan. I had a teen romance with Carole Gibson that was short but sweet! My respect for the Regulars runs deep; they were just like me, Philly kids who just wanted to do what they loved.

My life has had many twists and turns since the days when my career exploded on *American Bandstand*. I've traveled the world and performed for kings and queens, but those early days in that tiny TV studio that changed my world are never far from my heart. With deep love and affection to the *American Bandstand* dancers who made America smile.

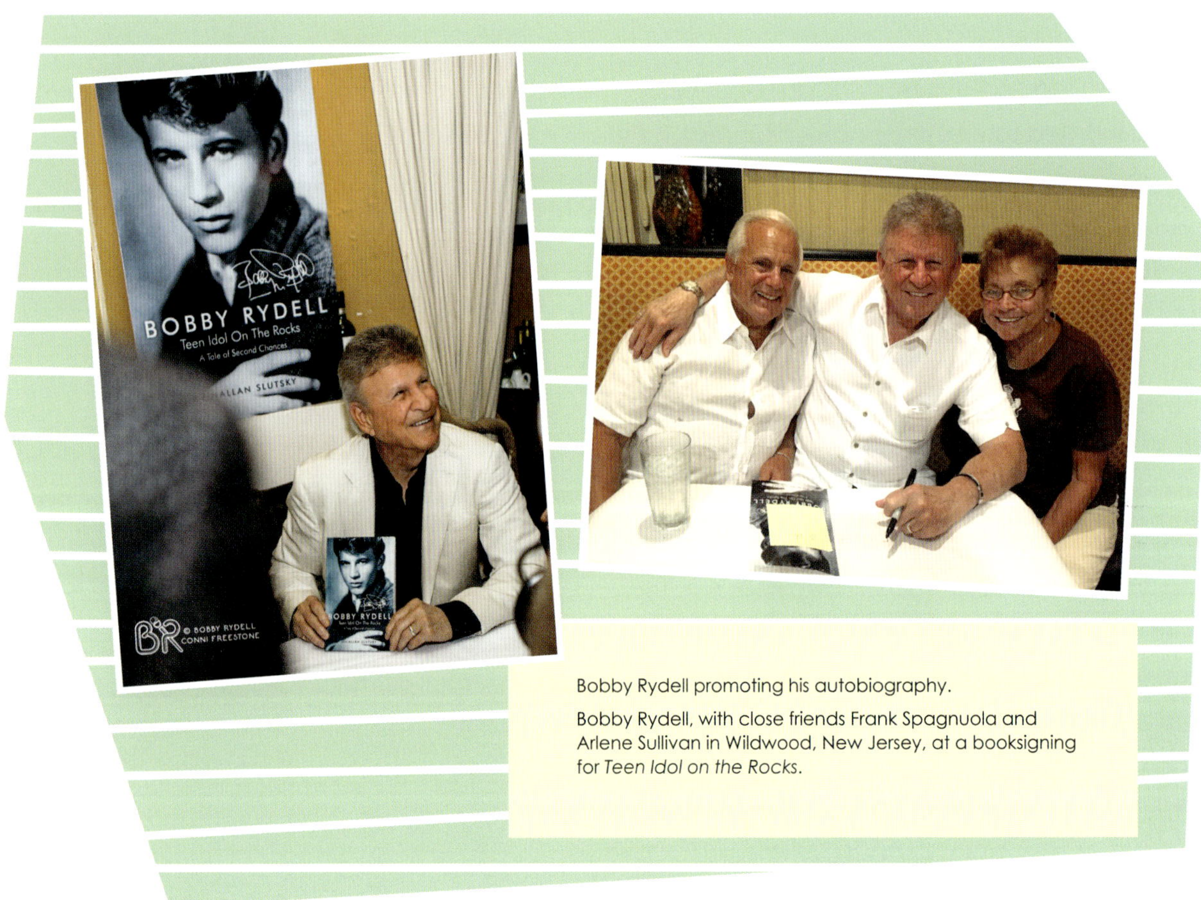

Bobby Rydell promoting his autobiography.

Bobby Rydell, with close friends Frank Spagnuola and Arlene Sullivan in Wildwood, New Jersey, at a booksigning for *Teen Idol on the Rocks*.

LOOKIN' BACK

Lookin' back and what do we see?
Images of what we all used to be;
Of times and events with its joy and tears,
Only traces remain of our high school years.
We're now so much older as we think what we did,
Back at the time when we all were just kids.
The words printed here are about me and you,
Filled with memories when everything was new,
Those times of our life, the way we were
Are locked in our treasury, safe and secure.
We know that those moments are forever past;
But by sharing together, we make them last.
Still and all, we're lookin' back to see what we can see,
And it warms the heart to touch those things of what we used to be.

—Al Koch

(Written for Al Koch's 25th High School Class Reunion, August 1983)

Rewinding to the 1950s

Chapter 1

Rewinding the Clock to 1957

While *Bandstand*, a local Philadelphia dance show, began to rule the television airwaves as *American Bandstand* in mid-1957, other events were also making headlines in the 48 states of America.

- 1957 is the biggest year of the Baby Boom, with one new baby born every seven seconds.
- This is the first year more people traveled by airplane than by train.
- The exodus to the suburbs explodes as more and more WWII vets take advantage of the GI Bill.
- 1,000 computers are sold in America.
- U.S. President Dwight D. Eisenhower announces a two-year suspension of nuclear testing.
- U.S. Senator Strom Thurmond (D-SC) sets the record for the longest filibuster with his 24-hour, 18-minute speech railing against a Civil Rights bill.
- Congress passes the Civil Rights Act of 1957, creating the Civil Rights Commission to, in part, investigate cases of African Americans being denied their right to vote in the South.
- Martin Luther King Jr. begins his battle against racial segregation.
- President Eisenhower sends federal troops to Little Rock Central High School to escort nine African-American children into school. Arkansas Governor Orval Faubus tries to block the students and stop integration.
- The Russians shock the world with their satellite Sputnik, the world's first artificial satellite, and it sparks the space race between the USSR and the USA.
- Leonard Bernstein's *West Side Story* opens on Broadway.
- 500 people die in Texas and Louisiana from Hurricane Audrey.

"The ideal modern woman married, cooked, and cared for her family, and kept herself busy by joining the local PTA and leading a troop of Campfire Girls. She entertained guests in her family's suburban house and worked out on the trampoline to keep her size 12 figure."

—*Life Magazine* (1956)

"The ideal 1950s man was the provider, protector, and the boss of the house."

—*Life Magazine* (1955)

The main concerns parents and teachers had with children in the 1950s:

- Being disrespectful
- Rising hemlines
- Juvenile delinquency
- Teenage drinking
- Breaking sexual rules
- The influence of rock 'n' roll
- The influence of comic books
- Polio

Teen Culture

By 1956, there were 13 million teens with $7 billion to spend annually. Teenagers in the 1950s were taught to obey authority, to be seen and not heard, and to control their emotions. We were also taught two don'ts: *Don't* make waves (fit in with the group!) and *Don't* even think about sex.

The Costs of Living in 1957[1]

- Average new house: $12,200
- Average monthly rent: $90
- Average yearly wages: $4,550
- Average cost of a car: $2,749
- A gallon of gas: 24 cents
- Bacon per pound: 60 cents
- Eggs per dozen: 28 cents
- Hi-Fi portable record player: $79.95
- 45 RPM record: 79 cents
- Movie tickets: 50 cents
- First-class stamps: 3 cents
- Children's shoes: $5.95

1 The People History, "The Year 1957," http://www.thepeoplehistory.com/1957.html.

Teens Remember

- Atomic bomb drills
- Polio shots
- Sock hops
- Drive-ins
- 45 RPM records
- Hot rods
- Crinolines
- Saddle shoes
- Circle pins
- Leather jackets

Average Annual Salaries

- Average: $4,550
- Secretary: $3,900
- Car Salesman: $7,000–$10,000

Share the fun... when you're with someone you like, it's fun to enjoy a Coke together. Good times get better with the best-loved sparkling drink in all the world! Coca-Cola ... so good in taste, in such good taste.

Coca-Cola SIGN OF GOOD TASTE

Television

- There were 47million sets in the USA.
- The RCA Victor model cost $78.
- *Leave It to Beaver*, *Perry Mason*, *Wagon Train*, and *Maverick* debut.

Popular Films

- *Around the World in Eighty Days*
- *12 Angry Men*
- *Jailhouse Rock*
- *The Bridge on the River Kwai*
- *The Three Faces of Eve*
- *An Affair to Remember*
- *Witness for the Prosecution*
- *A Face in the Crowd*
- *Funny Face*
- *The Incredible Shrinking Man*
- *Peyton Place*

Top Television Shows

- *Gunsmoke*
- *I Love Lucy*
- *The Ed Sullivan Show*
- *The Danny Thomas Show*
- *Have Gun Will Travel*
- *The Real McCoys*
- *I've Got a Secret*
- *Twenty One*
- *Wagon Train*

Popular Books

- *The Cat in the Hat* (Dr. Seuss)
- *From Russia with Love* (Ian Fleming)
- *The Guns of Navarone* (Alistair MacLean)
- *Please Don't Eat the Daisies* (Jean Kerr)
- *On the Road* (Jack Kerouac)

Memorable Songs

- *At The Hop* (Danny and the Juniors)
- *All Shook Up* (Elvis Presley)
- *Jailhouse Rock* (Elvis Presley)
- *You Send Me* (Sam Cooke)
- *Tammy* (Debbie Reynolds)
- *Diana* (Paul Anka)
- *Great Balls of Fire* (Jerry Lee Lewis)
- *School Day* (Chuck Berry)
- *Peggy Sue* (Buddy Holly)
- *Wake Up Little Suzie* (The Everly Brothers)

Also Stuck in our Minds

- Dinah Shore crooned "See the USA in Your Chevrolet" in television commercials
- Elvis Presley swiveled those hips in Jailhouse Rock and was "All Shook Up"
- Greyhound introduced its ad campaign: "It's such a comfort to take the bus and leave the driving to us."

New Inventions

- Stereo recordings
- Velcro
- Internal pacemakers
- Spandex
- AA size alkaline batteries produced for personal transistor radios
- Supermarkets introduce 5,000 new products… including frozen pizza

Popular Toys

- Slinkys
- Tonka toys
- Hula Hoops
- Model cars
- Frisbees
- Davey Crockett Coonskin caps

Also Remembering 1957… and Beyond

BY COOKIE HOROWITZ TISCHLER

Virgin pins; white pleated skirts; D.A. haircuts; dungarees; pop beads; I.D. bracelets; Bonomo's Turkish Taffy; playing potsy, jacks, red light green light, and stickball; voting for Miss Reingold, using baby oil and iodine as sun tan oil; the Beatles at Shea Stadium and Elvis on Ed Sullivan; the Plymouth Fury; *Ding Dong School*; Annette, Cubby, and Karen; kilt wrap skirts with decorative safety pins; the artichoke, beehive, and bubble hair styles; Arlene and Kenny, Carmen, Ivette, Justine and Bob; *Splendor in The Grass*; Mary Hartline; Ginny dolls; transistor radios; Nancy Drew; Robby Robot; Easy Bake ovens; Jingle Jump; Ouija boards; Bazooka bubble gum; Archie comics; air raid drills; Dep and hair wax; press-on nail polish and peel-off eyeliner; pettipants; sack and chemise dresses; rings on neck chains; white bucks; cap guns and air rifles; teacup monkeys advertised in the backs of comic books; Silhouettes; Winky Dink; Froggie the Gremlin; *Rootie Kazootie*; *Goin' To The Chapel*; *Soldier Boy*; Mr. Lee; Dr. Jonas Salk; Dr. Timothy Leary; banlon men's shirts; white go-go boots; topless swimsuits; fake IDs, Twiggy, copper P.O.W. bracelets; elephant bell bottoms and stove-pipe pants; gauze dresses and head wraps; poison rings; love beads; sit-ins and be-ins; Woodstock; leisure suits; platform shoes; jumpsuits; torn sweatshirts; shoulder pads; and a trillion more…

American Bandstand

By Albert Koch

American Bandstand made its ABC Television Network debut on August 5, 1957; by the time my senior year began less than a month later at Whiting High School in Indiana, my teenage classmates and I were avid fans. This five-day-a-week hop came to us live from Philadelphia in living black and white. Hosted by Dick Clark, *American Bandstand* presented the current heartthrobs of the record business, played the hottest hit records, and focused on the world of teenagers.

In the beginning, critics panned the show, warning that flaunting rock 'n' roll would corrupt teenage minds and lead to social decline. Television executives snickered when *Bandstand*, a local show, was proposed as a national network show. They argued that no one would watch a "bunch of kids dancing." Critics were adamant that the program would be a colossal flop. Clark believed otherwise, and within a few weeks, several million teenagers proved him right.

Almost single-handedly, Clark elevated the status of teens and brought respectability to the world of adolescents. He also established the importance of teenagers as consumers. Recording artists, record producers, sponsors, and advertisers flocked to Clark's doorstep hoping for a chance to display and promote both their talents and their products on *American Bandstand*.

From its initial broadcast on August 5 to November 17, *American Bandstand* was a full two hours of dancing, interviews, chitchat, rate-a-record, fan mail, and music from 3 to 5 p.m. So strong were its ratings that ABC inserted newcomer Johnny Carson's *Do You Trust Your Wife?/Who Do You Trust?* in the middle of Clark's time slot at 3:30 p.m. *American Bandstand* returned to the network at 4 p.m. to air the remaining hour of the show.

American Bandstand quickly became the nation's teenage headquarters and general store, with Clark as its manager. In cities throughout the nation, the show's enthusiastic, energetic, and voracious audience of adolescents eagerly procured the merchandise. Every afternoon, the city streets echoed the anthem of *American Bandstand*, Les Elgart's "Bandstand Boogie." This was the signal for teens of all ages to tune in and check out what was happening with the Regulars.

We immediately made *American Bandstand* a part of our lives. Along with listening to the music, teens copied fads, adopted fashions, and learned new dances from watching the Regulars. Kids across America selected their favorite personalities from the show and sent them fan letters and gifts.

Those of us too shy or timid for such public idolization privately savored the sights and sounds of America's daily dance party. Thousands of teenage girls swooned over Bob Clayton and wished they were his dance partner instead of Justine Carrelli. Bob and Justine became the show's sweethearts. Charter members of the eat-your-heart-out club were the guys who envied Kenny Rossi every time he slow danced with Arlene Sullivan.

A collection of 1950s memorabilia. Friends traveling across the United States would send Al Koch symbolic treasures that now fill glass cabinets and everywhere else in his downstairs rec room.

More memorabilia in Suzie and Al Koch's rec room.

Early 1960s phone booth with pay phone. In this phone booth, callers originally paid five cents to make a local call. For long distance, you called the operator, who told you how much money it would cost for three minutes of time. The operator chimed in when your three minutes were almost up to tell you how much to deposit for the next three minutes. If you didn't enter the coins fast enough, the operator might end your call.

Danny Turro driving his two-seater 1957 Ford Thunderbird, one of the most desirable cars in the antique car market. It originally sold for $3,043, and its top speed is 125 mph.

Danny Turro in the 1950s.

Facebook. I created a Dick Clark and *American Bandstand* group two years ago; it has grown so fast that we already have over 4,500 members!

> "*American Bandstand* was the Baby Boom generation's social network, our virtual community, the place where we enjoyed, vicariously, the companionship of dancers we could only watch on our TV screens."
>
> —Cheri Register, author
> www.cheriregister.com

Future Philly DJ Jerry Blavat dancing the day away in a spotlight dance on Bob Horn's *Bandstand*. Notice the girls in the bleachers wearing all those crinolines!

It's Just Kids Dancing

Chapter 2

It's Just Kids Dancing

By Ray Smith

There was a time when radio was king of the world. During its "golden age" in the 1930s and 1940s, families gathered around their radios to listen to dramas, soap operas, comedies, news shows, and live music. Around 1950, a small screen phenomenon called television toppled the king. Within two years, almost all of those popular shows and their sponsors migrated *en masse* to television. To survive, the endangered radio industry turned to recorded music.

Without national shows, stations were forced to create their own shows. Radio became local, and local meant regional. Suddenly, the airwaves were alive with country and western music, rhythm and blues, rockabilly, gospel, and pop. Local stations developed personalities to play, choose, and guide the music. This was the birth of the disc jockey. No longer just a host, the DJ would mirror and influence the emerging youth culture.

The two most popular radio shows in Philadelphia in the early 1950s were WPEN's *950 Club* and *Bob Horn's Bandstand* on WFIL. Both shows catered to the growing teen audience's desire to find its own music, its own voice. The *950 Club* featured interviews with musical guests and teenagers dancing in the studio to the latest pop records, which still largely reflected the past. Hosts Joe Grady and Ed Hurst made the teens an integral part of the show by talking to them about music, school, and their personal lives, so that listeners got to know them.

Bob Horn also played the latest records on his *Bandstand* program, but he was one of the few white DJs in the country to play rhythm and blues. Horn, like Alan Freed in Cleveland, knew that a growing number of the post–World War II generation identified more with the rebellious, sexually suggestive

The cover of the official 1955 *"Bandstand" Yearbook* shows Bob Horn with some of his loyal local regulars when the show was first televised only in the Philadelphia area.

Dancers pose in front of Bob Horn's podium and point to its list of the top 10 tunes. Remember the McGuire Sisters, Somethin' Smith & The Redheads, Alan Dale, Kay Starr, and Perry Como? They were some of the top singers and groups back in the day—July 1955.

It's just kids dancing on *Bandstand*, where guys didn't have the dress code that they did when the show transformed into *American Bandstand* and they had to wear jackets.

music of rhythm and blues than with the mellow love songs of Frank Sinatra and Glenn Miller. Freed, borrowing from a black euphemism for sex, called the "new" music rock 'n' roll.

By 1952, one in three American homes had a TV set. The youngest network, ABC, was barely formed yet. It had sporadic evening programming, and no daytime programming whatsoever; consequently, daytime programming was left to individual stations. WFIL-TV filled its afternoons with little-known old movies. Hardly anyone watched. Walter Annenberg, the owner of WFIL-TV and radio, didn't like that, and demanded that things change. It's not clear who recommended a teen dance show, though Annenberg takes credit, but general manager Roger Clipp and stations manager

George Koehler thought it was a great idea.

WFIL-TV was the home of ABC's *Paul Whiteman's TV Teen Club*. Each Saturday night, Whiteman featured teens dancing to live music, as well as a weekly talent competition. That competition spawned Charlie Gracie, Frankie Avalon, Dion, and an eight-year-old Leslie Uggams. Despite the success of Whiteman's show and the *950 Club*, the concept for WFIL's new teen show did not include dancing teens, or any teens at all. Nevertheless, Clipp immediately thought the hosts of the *950 Club* would be a perfect fit; but WPEN refused to let Grady and Hurst out of their contracts. Bob Horn, who the powers that be thought too dour and cold, was their reluctant choice; but Horn didn't care what choice he was; he was chomping at the bit for a television career.

Host Bob Horn leading the daily roll call on *Bandstand*. Kids gave their ages and said which school they attended.

Horn would play new records on the show, but to keep him from playing too much "jitterbug" (i.e., black) music, he was forced to fill most of the time with Snaders and Official Musical Films. These three- and four-minute films were precursors to today's music videos, but they lacked imagination and production values. They also featured such bygone artists as Bing Crosby and Cab Calloway.

Although the thirty-six-year-old Horn was one of the top DJs in the city, the managers thought his personality could never carry the show. He needed a co-host, they said. To soften him, and give the show some pizzazz, they hired the short, bespectacled local Muntz TV pitchman Lee Stewart. Stewart would not only bring levity to *Bandstand*, he would also bring the Muntz account to the fledgling station.

Bob Horn's Bandstand premiered in mid-September 1952. Within two weeks, it was yanked from the schedule. The show was a bomb, a total disaster. Horn, though, believed in it. He knew it could work with a little tweaking. The station gave him two weeks to reinvent the show. The first things to go were those dreadful music films. Then, he, like the others, emulated the *950 Club,* and invited teens in to dance.

Tony Mammarella, the show's producer, came up with a new set that suggested the inside of a 1940s music store. *Paul Whiteman's TV Teen Club* had used such a music store backdrop; it was appropriated for *Bandstand*. A podium set up in front of the backdrop suggested a store counter behind which Horn and Stewart would preside over the dance party. On the podium would be the name of the show, and the top ten records in the Delaware Valley. High school pennants would be hung to show the wide scope of the broadcast; and to make the studio more teen friendly, they brought in sliding wooden bleachers to mimic a gymnasium. The stage was set.

Since the WFIL-TV studios were within walking distance of three high schools, Horn believed an afternoon audience was guaranteed. Nevertheless, to pump up enthusiasm for the upcoming show, WFIL advertised heavily in all the local papers, including Annenberg's *The Philadelphia Inquirer*. Finally, on October 7, 1952, at 2:45 p.m., the reinvented *Bob Horn's Bandstand* opened its doors to the public. Unfortunately, few walked in.

Bob Crosby's *High Society* opened the show to an empty studio; Horn, Stewart, and Mammarella thought they might have been wrong in assuming they were guaranteed an audience. Then, just around 3 p.m., two girls from West Catholic High School, which was around the corner, meandered in. Within ten minutes, twenty-one kids were dancing; and finally, at 4 p.m., the audience had swelled to forty girls and ten boys. Taking a cue from the hosts of the *950 Club*, Horn moved to the floor to talk to the dancers; Blanche McCleary was the first teen ever interviewed on *Bandstand*.

By the third day, it was evident the station's advertising campaign had worked; at least one thousand kids lined up outside the studios at 46th and Market Streets. The new show was an instant hit. Joe Grady noted the show's sudden success, saying, "Bob Horn stole our show right out from under us. He's raped us and it's legal!"

Studio B only held 200 people, so to accommodate the hundreds who wanted in, they rotated the audience. The first group would be on from 2:45 to 4 p.m., and the second group from 4 to 5 p.m. Horn always considered the kids to be the stars of the show; in order to give them a greater sense of participation, he created the roll call, the record review, and the spotlight dance.

Horn also organized a "committee" made up of the dancers; this would guarantee not only the Regulars' participation in the show, but also a daily audience. He handpicked the first twenty members, giving them membership cards, and asking them to pledge they'd be at the studio, no matter what the weather. The committee members soon began referring to themselves as the Regulars. By the end of first month, there were forty Regulars who no longer had to wait in line, and could stay for the entire show.

When he was only twelve years old (two years below the age limit), Jerry Blavat snuck into the show. He was soon dancing there every day. Horn recognized Blavat as an asset; even though he

The Canadian quartet, The Crew Cuts, was one of many musical groups who lip-synced their hit songs on both *Bandstand* and *American Bandstand*. Their name reminded fans of the popular haircut many male teens had at the time. The Crew Cuts were known for such mid-1950s hits as "Sh-Boom" ("Life Could Be a Dream"), "Unchained Melody," and "Earth Angel."

was underage, Blavat was asked to be on the committee, which he would soon earn fifteen dollars a week to head. Blavat would also help Horn choose which records would be good for the weekly feature, record review (which later became rate-a-record).

Although the show was a big success, not everyone was pleased; suggestions abounded on how to make it better. The funniest allegedly came from Walter Annenberg's wife, Lee. She thought the kids were too shabbily dressed and suggested the boys wear tuxes and the girls wear pretty party dresses. Someone suggested they wear theatrical makeup to hide teenage blemishes. Since so many older people loathed the music of this new generation, they suggested Horn play more music from the 1930s, like Glenn Miller. Fortunately, none of these suggestions were accepted.

One suggestion, however, was implemented in 1955. Tony Mammarella told the management that *Bandstand* was "not a two-man show." Stewart, who never got along with Horn, and who never really brought much levity to the show, was let go. He did not fade gently into the night, however; Stewart was given his own morning show, *Lee Stewart's Coffeetime*, a morning version of *Bandstand*, but without age limits, and with more Glenn Miller. It lasted only a few months. Bob Horn finally had the spotlight to himself.

Bandstand was on a roll; in 1956, its audience was growing, its sponsors were happy, and Horn was raking in big money. However, management was growing increasingly frustrated with Horn. They thought him arrogant, moody, and, at forty, too old for a youth-oriented show. If they ever wanted to pitch the show to the network, they said, they needed a younger host. In the wings, they had the baby-faced, clean-cut, twenty-five-year-old Dick Clark. Clark had subbed for Horn once, and he regularly did live commercials on the show. He knew the terrain. He was ready for his moment.

There's much speculation about how Horn's life spiraled downward so quickly. Suffice to say, much of his downfall was self-inflicted. On June 21, 1956, Horn was arrested on a DUI; he was immediately taken off the air. Mammarella replaced him while he worked out his legal problems.

Bob Horn was enormously popular with the kids on the show; they did not want to see him go, but Mammarella told Jerry Blavat that Horn was out, and Dick Clark would be taking over the show permanently. On July 9, 1956, the day that Clark was to start hosting the show, Blavat led a protest by the show's Regulars outside the studio. They demanded that Bob Horn be reinstated. Dick Clark, wanting to defuse the situation, offered to double Blavat's fifteen dollar "salary" if he would come back to the show and persuade the others to follow him. Blavat, who was loyal to Horn, refused and walked away from the show forever. *Bandstand* went on that day with the Regulars in the studio and Dick Clark at the podium—where he would remain for more than thirty-three years.

In November 1956, Horn was indicted on charges of statutory rape and corrupting a minor. He was tried twice on the charges; the first trial ended in a hung jury. The second jury acquitted him. Ironically, the reporter for the *Courier-Post* was Horn's former co-host, Lee Stewart. With Horn's career all but over, he began drinking heavily; on January 22, 1957, he drove the wrong way on a one-way street, injuring five people, one of them seriously. Bob Horn served six months in jail. He moved to Texas and changed his name to Bob Adams. He died in 1966 of a heart attack while mowing his lawn. Bob Horn, the creator of *Bandstand,* was just fifty years old.

"I remember the day I came down those el steps and had about seven Regulars waiting for me—to take me into *Bandstand* with Bob Horn. I was nervous and felt like I was auditioning all over again. Best times of my life. It was a sad day when we arrived that one day and were told that Bob had been replaced by Dick Clark. We had no idea what the reason was. We picketed the show that day. A week or so later the Regulars went back on and some remained until Dick took the show to California—a sad day for us and a sad day for Philadelphia."

—Lenny Cooney

Dick Clark always thought of himself as a salesman. From his earliest days at WFIL-TV and Radio in Philadelphia, Dick pitched products from candy to Clearasil to CDs.

The Rise of a Salesman

Chapter 3

Pictures taken at Dick Clark's American Bandstand Grill, King of Prussia, PA, on its last day open (5/24/03).

and remained a force in the entertainment industry all his life. He was inducted into the Rock and Roll Hall of Fame in 1993. In 2004, Clark revealed that he had type 2 diabetes. Later that year, he suffered a stroke, which affected his speech permanently. In April 2012, America's oldest teenager died during surgery at the age of eighty-two.

> On *American Bandstand,* "Stars were born, fads were hatched, and a group of typical American kids danced their way into the hearts of all the show's viewers."
>
> —Steve Brandt, *16 Magazine*

The dance floor is busy—and so is Dick Clark, speaking with the control room on his telephone during a dance number.

Dancing on AIR

Chapter 4

Dancing on Air

By Ray Smith

Dancing was a way of life in Philadelphia, or at least it was in my life. I was nine years old when I went to my first dance at the Police Athletic League; but I'd been dancing around the house with my mother, a failed marathon dancer, since I could stand on my own. If my mother had had her way, I would have stayed my entire life in Philadelphia dancing with her in the living room. I didn't want that, so going to a dance, or to *Bandstand,* was essential; like many Philadelphia teens, going to *Bandstand* at least once was a rite of passage. *Bandstand* wasn't just another dance; for many it was an escape route. I remember my first days on the show as if it were only a week ago; perhaps a few years ago, I might have remembered it like it was yesterday, but I'm in my seventies now, and, as I am learning, time plays tricks on memory. Sometimes we remember things that never happened, and sometimes we remember moments we wished had happened, but never did. There is an element of fiction in all memory.

Anyway, that first day was hot, abnormally hot, even for Philadelphia. It was late July and the temperature in late morning hovered in the mid-90s; the humidity was just as high. I was standing on Market Street in a dark brown wool jacket, a long sleeve shirt with black onyx cuff links, and a cheap striped tie. About thirty other teenage boys stood beside me in line against the wall of the WFIL-TV and Radio Studios. We were waiting to get into Philadelphia's number one afternoon TV dance party, *Bandstand*. Sweat poured off my forehead and down the back of my neck. The scent of Aqua Velva faded with it. Some of us hugged the wall, trying to squeeze into a narrow slice of shade for relief. My eyes roamed the crowd. They stopped on a boy with pale blue eyes, a wide toothy grin, and red hair that fell quietly onto his freckled face. Sometimes you look at someone, and you know instantly you want to be with him (or for some, her). I wanted to be with a lot of boys, but I'd never been with any. Not one! Maybe this day would be different.

Even with red hair, he looked dangerous. I liked that. I heard someone call him Mickey. The name fit. I couldn't take my eyes off him, but I was afraid he might catch me staring. I kept turning away, watching him, turning away again, and then watching him again from the corner of my eye.

I closed my eyes; I felt his arm around my shoulder. I could taste cigarettes on his lips, an odd taste that I would grow to hate. But on this hot July day, I loved it. An el train passed overhead, creating a cacophony of noise and music. My eyes popped open. I caught Mickey looking at me; our eyes locked for a fleeting moment. I panicked. I turned my attention back to the red doors that lead to the studio. My brain was muddled. I concentrated on the heat. I sang a song in my head. I tried to relax, but I couldn't. I knew, however, that within a matter of minutes I would be inside Studio B, where the air was considerably cooler, and exceedingly rare. I would be on *Bandstand*.

The entire city would soon see me; perhaps even my family would see me, though I seriously doubt my parents or anyone in my family would be watching television in the afternoon except maybe for *Queen for a Day*. Besides, my family rarely saw anything I did. My mom never saw me in a school play or met a teacher on parent-teacher night. My dad, on the other hand, saw everything; he took me everywhere, but he never commented on anything. He was a blank page on which I wrote many things.

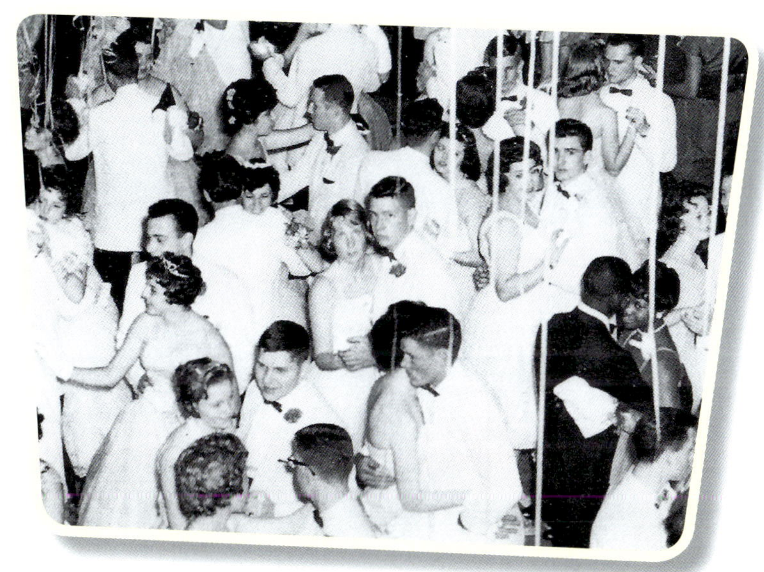

White sports coats and pink carnations fill the gym for Bartram High School's Spring Formal for seniors, 1960

The anticipation of getting into the show that day apparently agitated the brood of butterflies inhabiting my stomach. I was restless. My mind jumped all over the place—sometimes on Mickey, sometimes on the show, sometimes on the red doors. Why was I so nervous? I'd been in Studio B before on *Lee Stewart's CoffeeTime*. Stewart was this short, nerdy-looking fellow with a round face, and round horned-rimmed glasses. He and the studio chiefs had the mistaken belief that he was funny and would bring some levity to the show. He was not, and he did not! He had been co-host of *Bandstand* alongside the show's creator, Bob Horn, since the show debuted in 1952; but the partnership was beyond abysmal, and Horn demanded Stewart be ousted. However, Stewart brought with him a huge sponsor, and the station management could not afford to lose one of its biggest moneymakers. So, as too often happens in television, they gave him his own show, *CoffeeTime*.

CoffeeTime was a morning version of *Bandstand,* in the same studio with the same bleachers, and many of the same records, but unlike *Bandstand* it didn't have age limits. Otherwise, I never

Ray Smith, age 13, hanging out on his front steps and looking cool on a hot summer's day in 1955.

would have been allowed on; I was only twelve, and my cousin Julie whom I went with, was eleven. We secretly arranged to meet one morning and go to the show. We told our parents we were going to the library; parents are sometimes just extraordinarily gullible (at least ours were). Julie's mom would never have allowed her to dance on television had she known. She was a strict, intolerant Irish Catholic woman who believed dancing led innocent children to sex. I hoped she was right—I sometimes prayed she was right—perhaps that's why I went to so many dances. But it never happened. I always went home alone.

Anyway, Julie and I caught the bus, took a short ride on the el, and joined the line outside the building at 46th and Market Streets. Our parents had no clue we were going to be dancing on a television show, especially because we were so young. Julie didn't want to lie to her mother, but I told her that lying to parents was necessary to teenage life. She remained reluctant; she knew I was a ham and that's why we were going. My nickname was "Hammy." I craved attention, but in a quiet way. I wrote plays and acted out movies in the light on my basement wall from my movie projector. More often than not, I got attention through my dancing. Julie and I were damn good dancers; she knew how to follow me perfectly. I was the one who needed to show off. She was, simply put, a vehicle for me. Wow, how cruel does that sound? It didn't seem so cruel at the time.

Unfortunately, a crowd of elderly housewives dancing together overshadowed us on the *CoffeeTime* dance floor (considering our ages, the women were probably in their thirties and forties;

they seemed elderly to us). I don't remember more than a handful of men on the show ever. Dancing amongst these ladies was like dancing at one of my parents' parties; the only things missing were the drunks and the arguments. These women were definitely more into Tony Bennett and Patti Page than Elvis Presley and Frankie Lymon. Julie and I danced on *CoffeeTime* weekly that summer, but we never told anyone about it. It became just another part of my secret life.

I had been in the line outside this studio before, but this time was different; everything was simultaneously familiar and unfamiliar. It's like going to the circus—you know you're going to see clowns and elephants, but when you see them, it's as if you'd never seen them before and they're magic all over again. I didn't tell my cousin that I was going to *Bandstand*. I wanted to be alone. I didn't tell anyone, especially my parents, that I was going. I knew by the time I got home my parents probably wouldn't be home yet. I was counting on that.

I was a latchkey kid who came home from school every day to an empty house; this outrages experts on television today. I loved it; I could be free. I had hours to pretend. I could be anywhere I dreamed of and be anything I wanted to be. Sometimes, I made costumes using the living room curtains. I just loved the feeling of the fabric against my body. I know that sounds odd, but I wanted something touching me; fabric worked just fine. Being alone in line, I hoped I could meet someone new, someone who might like me the way I wanted to like him. Of course, I'd never been seriously into anyone in real life. I was only fifteen. Oh, I was into Roy Rogers, and into a neighborhood kid named Bobby because he had Roy's eyes, those narrow slits. But other than wrestling with each other, nothing serious happened.

After more than an hour in the heat, I questioned the sanity of being there at all. Nevertheless, I persevered and stood there suffering silently, obsessing about the heat and Mickey. I caught him staring at me, and for a nanosecond our eyes locked; I turned away, terrified that he'd caught me doing something wrong, something dirty. I looked toward the girls' line and was distracted by some of the stars of the show: Joanne MonteCarlo and Tom DeNoble walked past us and right into the building through those two big red doors. Little Ro, in her black-and-white saddle shoes, waved and said hi to some girls; she, too, walked right into the studio. Those three were Regulars; they didn't have to wait in no stinkin' line like the rest of us. Watching them, I fantasized that someday I would be a Regular and would probably ignore the crowd, too.

A long time passed; and the wait stretched into its second hour. The temperature now verged on one hundred degrees. My wet shirt had become part of my back. I wanted to take my jacket off. I wanted every guy in line to take his clothes off. Everyone was fidgety. Some boys left the line and lit up cigarettes even though it was forbidden. They were the tough guys from South Philadelphia; they knew how to smoke. I glanced constantly at the studio doors, hoping the doorman's head would pop out and invite us in and save me from Mickey's judgment. Then, with our nerves fraying, a tall, portly fellow in a wrinkled, ill-fitting checkered jacket appeared. He looked friendly and was smiling. The time had finally come to enter the "promised land."

Then came the bombshell: "Not everyone will get in today," he said, still smiling. I was at the front of the line, and I knew if he saw me, he'd say, "Come in, young man; we need you." I was, after all, paler than most of the others in line. Dark-haired Italian kids dominated the show. I was a dusty blond, clean-cut—an all-American youth of no discernable ethnic origin; I didn't even identify as being Polish. The show wasn't worried about "type." Anyway, I was silly to worry, because *all* the boys got in; the girls were not so lucky, even though they way outnumbered us. The show needed guys, otherwise the girls would be dancing with each other a lot, which they did anyway.

That really bugged me. How come they can dance with each other, and I can't dance with, say, Mickey, who was now standing next to me? I saw how well built he was, his luminous eyes shining and mysterious, and his ginger pompadour now rivaling the Sierra Nevadas. I danced with him in my head; but I would have been thrown off the show in two seconds if I had even suggested or joked about dancing with him. It was a homophobic world long before we knew what that meant. The doorman politely ushered us into this homophobic world, telling us to wait in the hall. Another line. To be a part of any TV audience, you have to wait endlessly in lines. I stood there grinning from ear to ear, happy just thinking of where I was and what was about to happen.

Walking into Studio B was like walking from Kansas into Oz. It was unlike anything I knew on the outside: the lights, the smell, the strange dead sound, and even the walls, resembled nothing in my daily world. Studio B was an artificial, hermetically sealed world—like Oz. Beyond the cinderblock walls, Sputnik was soaring through space and blacks were demanding their place in our space, but inside, Little Richard and Sam Cooke beguiled us with songs of puppy love and sexual desire. Despite our parents' denial, and to their great dismay, these were the very things we teenagers thought about most of the time. Well, *I* thought about them most of the time. I tried to think of other things, but today being around so many guys that seemed more like me than the boys in my neighborhood, it was impossible. I confess that I felt paranoid, scared that someone might figure out what I was thinking or catch me staring; how could I explain that to my parents? I looked calm on the outside, but inside I was exploding. Nevertheless, I felt privileged being inside the studio; I was, after all, a part of something that most people would never, and could never, be a part of.

It was intoxicating knowing strangers were watching me. But everyone my age, inside and outside the studio, was part of something big; we just didn't know it yet. When you're in the middle of something, you rarely know it's the middle of something; it's just another moment in your life. As you age, you realize that life is just a series of such moments. And memories, after all, are just moments recalled. In 1957, we were on the cusp of changing the world forever; we were "teenagers," a new subclass of consumers that sprang up after World War II. We were a group that was never singled out before. Perhaps most important, we had money, lots of money, and we were spending it in unprecedented amounts, especially on records and entertainment. My three-dollar weekly allowance was going to 45 RPM records and dances. Madison Avenue created us, and Dick Clark grasped our importance immediately, which shouldn't be surprising because he was about commerce more than anything

John Bartram High School prom night, 1959. Dressed in their formal attire, Dottie Hill and Ray Smith are ready to head off to the Benjamin Franklin Hotel for their big night at the Senior Prom. Ms. Hill is wearing an expansive string of white carnations on her wrist.

else. He was first and foremost a businessman. He saw music as business, not art.

Well, whatever cusp we were on, we weren't cusping that day. I inched into the studio with the other guys and immediately felt relief, even though it was a chilling thirty-something degrees in there. The thick, drab curtains covering the walls embraced me like an army blanket on a cold winter night. I felt anxiously at ease. The high school pennants on the far wall and the bleachers were a reminder that I was still in high school. The bleachers took up most of the space, shrinking the size of the dance floor by more than half. Rows of big, black, dusty lights hung from the ceiling, and when they were on, they felt like sunlight. It was unreal. They took the room from freezing to tolerable.

The most unique thing in the room was the sound; it sat flat in my ear with no echoes or resonance. It felt like what it must be like inside a jar with the lid screwed on. No sounds of the outside world infiltrated this space; Market Street and the noisy el disappeared. I was definitely somewhere else. But just as I lost myself in the strangeness of the room, Tony Mammarella, the show's producer and Clark's righthand man, interrupted us to explain how things worked, and what was expected of us. As he spoke, I searched the bleachers for Mickey. I thought he would have followed me up to the top, but he didn't. I wondered if he even knew where I was. Had he noticed me? Probably not. That made me want him all the more. I continued my search, listening to Tony.

Tony pointed to the white line on the dance floor, and told us that we had to stay on one side of it; violate that rule and you were out. He told us to be careful of the cameras, which were bulky and attached to miles of thick black cables. Then, perhaps the biggest rule of all, "Do not look into the cameras. Pretend they're not there," he explained. "This is a party, and the people at home are eavesdropping on us." What an exciting thought. That one simple rule, however, was the rule the Regulars continuously broke. When the cameras were near and the little red light atop them was ablaze, these kids were like moths to a flame. But, that's probably why I recognize them; they are always visible.

The Regulars all but ignored Tony—talking amongst themselves, sharing fan letters, and primping for the cameras as he spoke. I finally saw Mickey talking to one of the Regulars, a boy from West Catholic High School. They might be in the same class. They might be friends. He turned, and looking up, he saw me. He melted in my eyes. He didn't turn away. I didn't turn away either. I came down; he took my hand and danced with me. Bobby Darin's "Dream Lover" blasted through the studio. The guy beside me startled me into reality. "Have you been here before?" he asked. I didn't know what he was talking about. My daydream of Mickey, once again, disappeared. I said no.

I'm comfortable being a voyeur; my bravado usually fades into insecurity and shyness. Consequently, I was sitting high up in the bleachers where I could participate in the show without participating. I was watching the pageant unfold before me. I loved watching how people moved and acted. I fantasized about moving and acting with them. I wanted to be a star, but if I were beside a movie star, or talking to a star, that meant that I was somebody, and that was okay.

I watched how the kids were dancing and who was dancing with whom. Dancing, as I said, is second nature to us; it's a familiar ritual. And it's partner dancing here. We all do it. We hold the girl's waist with our right hand and the girl's right hand in our left hand. We glide around the dance floor counterclockwise. I laugh when I see today's kids slow dance; they barely move. I wouldn't even call it dancing. You'd never know they were moving to music. Maybe they're just into each other's bodies. That was forbidden for us, even though Dick once said slow dancing was sex standing up and with your clothes on. When we jitterbugged—and everyone in Philadelphia did—we knew the steps and rhythms of the dance. Each neighborhood had little variations, but we all knew the basics. It was the same with the Chalypso (a Philadelphia dance) or the Strand, a dance introduced by *Bandstand* dancers, but created by dancers on another Philadelphia dance show, *The Mitch Thomas Show*, a weekly black version of *Bandstand*.

Dick Clark fascinated me. I can't explain it; he just did. I saw him all the time on TV pitching jewelry for Barr's Jewelers, the place where most high school seniors bought their class rings. I never believed him; he seemed insincere to me. He reminded me of a cross between the super clean-cut Pat Boone and my equally clean-cut Uncle Harry. Harry was a handsome, square-jawed former sailor with hazel eyes. He was tall and muscular. He never needed a shave. I love looking at the pictures of him in uniform. I spent part of my summers with Harry and my Aunt Bea. Harry may have been pretty, but he was a tyrant who beat and tortured us. Was Clark a tyrant when the cameras were off? I didn't know. He was a mystery that only existed in a two-dimensional image. Was he close to any dancers?

With so many things to look at, I turned my attention away from Mickey and to Clark.

Clark walked into the studio carrying a dark briefcase and papers. He was shorter than I imagined; he was lean, and dressed in dull grey. He was as colorless as the drapes. He looked as if he were going to work in a bank. His hair was neatly parted and held in place by a generous application of Vitalis; it wasn't as greasy as some other hair stuff, like the stuff that a lot of the South Philadelphia boys used to create big pompadours.

Crossing in front of the bleachers, he barely acknowledged anyone, even though some of the Regulars greeted him enthusiastically. He was careful about mingling. He didn't want to cross over that white line. Clark's predecessor, Bob Horn, was fired after accusations of statutory rape (Horn was in his mid-forties) and alcohol abuse. Clark was determined to counter that image with an image of clean-cut, sexless teenagers, as well as an asexual all-American host; this was smart because Clark knew it was the only way adults would accept his program, as well as rock 'n' roll, which most adults feared, believing it promoted juvenile delinquency.

So, fearful of the kids' real behavior, he imposed a strict dress code: jackets and ties for boys, and nothing tight for girls. He promoted the couples on the show to mask the fact that so many guys were gay. He reportedly kept close tabs on the Regulars outside the studio. Someone told me (and I have no proof of this) that he had spies concentrated on Rittenhouse Square in the center of the city. It's a tony manicured park surrounded by townhouses, a hotel, and classy high-rise apartment buildings; its benches are always full; and it had long been a meeting place for gays. It's a cruising park for the affluent. It also attracts a lot of young gays because it's far away from their neighborhoods.

I walked through it a couple of times, scared but hopeful. I met no one; I never even spoke to anyone. I didn't know about the so-called spies. The irony about Clark is he was not the goody-two-shoes he projected: he smoked, cursed, and for a while teetered on the edge of alcoholism. But to his credit and diligence, he brilliantly created his own myth, and he stuck to it for the rest of his life. I think after several decades he actually believed the myth. The ancient Greeks said that everyone wears a mask, and that as we grow older we grow into our mask. In those early days of *Bandstand*, Clark was trying on his mask. He was a cool professional with an agenda from the beginning, an agenda for success that made him rich; he was a millionaire by the end of the 1950s. Clark was a cool person, and not cool meaning hip. One Regular described him as "friendly, but not too friendly." When he spoke to us off-screen, it was usually from the podium; it gave him command over his domain, and as I have learned over the years, Clark liked and wanted to be in command.

Most TV studios are far smaller than they appear on the television screen (having worked in television for almost fifty years, I know this to be true) and Studio B was no exception. It was cramped, especially as the cameras crept about. The space was divided into areas: the bleachers, Clark's podium, the chipped autograph desk, the performance area with its cheap curtains, and the forbidden area behind the white line where the cameras and monitors sat. Because the room was so contained and soundproofed, the music was often deafeningly loud, which to my teenage ears was the best and only way to listen to rock 'n' roll; it knocked everything else out of your head. But sometimes over the music, Clark's voice, even louder, invaded the room, ordering some of the Regulars (often Arlene, Frani, and Carole) to move away from the cameras and go to the back of the dance floor. Occasionally, when annoyed by their antics, Clark told them to leave for the day or even the week. They're goofy teenagers; he's strict and doesn't like goofiness.

Between records, Clark was always on the phone or running to do a commercial. He was a man in constant motion. Clark was only twelve years older than I, yet he felt like a "full-grown" adult, not quite like my mom and dad, but like an older brother or uncle. Girls and mothers fawned over him. I'm sure a few guys did too; I didn't. I never found him attractive. He was nice-looking, but for me, his head was too big for his body. He was too shiny, too squeaky clean. My secret desire, as I mentioned, was Mickey, who had danger lurking beneath the fire atop his head. But, like Clark, I kept everything, including my desires, at a safe distance, buried deep inside.

I decided I wouldn't be asking anyone to dance that day. Even though I *knew* I was a great dancer, I was self-conscious about asking a stranger to dance because of my slight speech impediment. Since elementary school, I had trouble with the letters *r* and *s* (a lot like Barbara Walters). I went to speech therapy, and by the time of *Bandstand*, I had pretty much conquered the problem; but I feared that if excited, I would lapse into sibilant s's, branding myself before a TV audience as a "fairy" or "fruit," or a "fellow too light for his loafers."

While that was churning in my head, my feet were pounding the seat in front of me, keeping the beat to Lavern Baker or The Coasters. I was swaying all over the place, and couldn't sit still. I needed to get out of the bleachers, which were uncomfortably firm. In a moment of complete abandon, I bolted down the bleachers onto the equally hard cement dance floor, which was murder on your feet; but it was a small price to pay for being seen dancing next to the Regulars. Remember, if I was seen beside the Regulars, people would think I was part of the spectacle. I swallowed my fears, prepared my tongue, and timidly asked "Peanuts," a young blonde girl in a pretty blue sweater and smelling of sweet Jean Naté, to dance. Without blinking an eye, she quietly, but politely, said, "Sorry." She smiled without separating her lips and walked away. She could've hit me with a sledgehammer in my chest; it would have hurt less. My heart stopped. I gasped for air. I felt like crying (I was such a girl). I felt hot scarlet blood oozing out of my punctured chest, running down my leg, and staining the gray dance floor, reminding the dancers Ray died there. With my shoulders slumped, I crawled back to my perch, and settled in for the rest of the show.

When I returned to the show at the end of that first week, I was determined to never feel the pain of rejection again; I brought my own dance partner, my friend Annie, and another friend from school, Jerry. We waited in separate lines outside the studio, hoping to get in. Annie didn't make the cut; so, surprising even myself, Jerry and I did the next best thing: we left the line. The three of us jumped on the el and headed over to *The 950 Club* at radio station WPEN.

Joe Grady and Ed Hurst were the hosts of this radio dance party. Yes, a radio version of *Bandstand*.

Ray Smith watching Dick Clark from the stands in the winter of 1956. Ginnie, his dance partner, is sitting to his right. Down in the first row Arlene is sitting next to Little Ro. It was Arlene's second week on the show. To Arlene's left, you can see Regular Myrna Horowitz, and above Ray is Regular Peggy Leonard. Arlene and Ray are so close, but it took them 40 years to meet.

Actually, it's the other way around. Bob Horn recreated what Grady and Hurst had on radio for his TV show *Bandstand*. I loved the Grady and Hurst studio because it was more like a luncheonette than a studio; in reality, it *was* a luncheonette, The Liberty Room. Apparently, when we left, the food and waitresses came out. Annie and I danced on the red-and-white square-tiled floor and met some other kids who had been turned away from *Bandstand*. We were a happy bunch, and for a while, we came to *The 950 Club* rather than trying to get on *Bandstand*. But *Bandstand* was bigger and more enticing; it was like a siren to my Odysseus.

When Clark took the show national on August 5, 1957, I realized that being on *American Bandstand* was about more than dancing. It was about being in a place where nobody knew me, somewhere away from my house, and away from the kids in my neighborhood. I wanted to escape everything familiar. I *had* to go back. Dumping Annie for the time being (seems to be a pattern, doesn't it?), I returned to the line. I thought Jerry might show up, but he didn't. I was alone.

It was the end of August, and Clark had made *American Bandstand* more popular than ever. It was still hot and the lines were even longer, but I didn't care. For whatever reason, I got in that day, and almost every time after that. *The 950 Club* melted away; it became another memory, another moment in another time. Now on *American Bandstand*, I stupidly repeated the mistake I made on *Bandstand*; I came down from the heavens, and with my heart racing, I asked Justine Carrelli—another blonde, and arguably the most popular girl on the show—to dance. (Chutzpah, huh?) I used to see her at a local dance, and thought she might recognize me from there. Foolish, foolish me! She turned me down faster than "Peanuts" had with a definite "I can't." It was obviously time for Annie again.

My parents never saw me on *Bandstand* or *American Bandstand*. The shows were live for three hours, every afternoon, five days a week; my parents were either sleeping or working. They didn't even know I was *on* the show. Some of the kids in my neighborhood, and a few at school, bullied me about being on the show. They called me "Mr. Bandstand," and in those days in Philadelphia, that was not always a compliment. The dancers were loved outside the city, but ridiculed and threatened inside the city. Boys were either jealous of us, or thought we were queer, which gave them reason to bully us and beat us up. I was made fun of, but never beaten. Jerry was pushed onto the el tracks, and Paul was hung over an elevator shaft. Personally, I didn't care what they called me. I was, for good or bad, "somebody" in their eyes. How sick was that? What can I say? I was a confused teenager.

I came to the show a few days every week those first months of *American Bandstand;* and after weeks of groveling before Clark, he finally picked me for the record review (not "rate-a-record," as it was called later in L.A.) the second week of December. In those days, three of us scored the records, and one averaged our scores. I remember one song of the three we heard that day —"Get a Job" by The Silhouettes. It became number one in 1958. I like to think I helped to make it a hit. And, oh yes, for being on record review we were given a Christmas gift: an LP of John Facenda (a local TV news announcer) reading the nativity story—just what every teenager wanted.

In December of 1957, I was chosen to be on the nighttime version of *American Bandstand,* which aired on Monday nights at 7:30 p.m. Because it was at night, I think they pushed back the bleachers and replaced them with tables. At least I don't remember bleachers (it's that thing about time and memory again). The studio was adorned for Christmas. A decorated tree stood in one corner, and some girls wore red and green ribbons in their hair; others wore these annoying bells on their ankles. My parents saw this show because they bought me a new suit for it. I was beaming when my father drove Annie and me to the studio. I felt older; but, as he reminded me, I was still fifteen years old. The show, however, never got older; it was cancelled after a few weeks. They discovered the afternoon audience was not tuning in at night; moms were cooking dinner, kids were doing homework, and dads simply did not want to watch a bunch of irritating teenagers dance to music they didn't like.

I became part of the *American Bandstand* soap opera in 1957, though, and make no mistake about this: I was a minor, *truly minor*, part of it. I was not known to the TV audience, and never received a single fan letter. I was never a Regular. I went to the show on and off, more off than on, until early 1960, always pretending that I was part of the show and not just a guest. I was a guest. I still had to wait in line, though I never got turned away again. I was committed to school, and in order to fit in there, I was on every possible committee, as well as one of the editors of the yearbook; I had little time to rush down to 46th and Market Streets, a considerable way from my high school, to make it to the studio in time (2:30 p.m.) for air. But I cherish all the times I was on the show. I watched and learned how a television studio worked, which would later help me in my career at NBC. I didn't get to dance with any of the Regulars, but I got to dance with some celebrities of that era: Janice Harper, Joni James, Jaye P. Morgan, Phyllis McGuire, and Gogi Grant among them (does anyone remember them?). And I think about this all the time: I was present at the birth of rock 'n' roll, in the city where it was centered, and on the show that introduced it to, and spread it across, the country.

I was part of the new teenage culture, and I shared my days with a national icon. That's pretty impressive. On top of all that, I lived out a dream: I was in my private version of show business. On another level, in the cloistered, homophobic world known as Studio B, I realized I was different—I had different aspirations than the kids in my neighborhood; I didn't think like my family; and, like many of the boys on *American Bandstand*, I realized I liked boys. Of course, that scared me a lot; some of the boys on the show scared me because I was attracted to them. I was only a teen, and was terrified to act on any of those feelings, so I created a fantasy life, and ultimately, a secret life. Had I been braver, I might have explored my sexuality with the boys on *American Bandstand* who were also exploring their desires. But I wasn't brave.

In my first year on *American Bandstand*, the outside and inside worlds were separate; but as time passed, dust collected on those colorless curtains, and the high school pennants came down. The wall separating those two worlds collapsed. Society was in flux. Morals were challenged. Traditions were scrapped. For the first time in history, we, teenagers, had power at the cash register, giving us power to change things. By the mid-1960s, we found our voice. And, to our credit, we used it. What a great time I had. What a great teenage life I lived. I liked the beat, and I danced to it.

The Real "American Bandstand"

BY ANONYMOUS

If you live far from Philadelphia, the city from where *American Bandstand* is broadcast, you can write in for reservations to be on the show. You might write in even if you are a local resident, though the chances of getting a reservation letter are very slim when you live nearby.

Otherwise, you can wait in line with hundreds of others, hoping to be one of the 150 guests chosen for each show. If it happens to be summer or a holiday, the line seems to be a mile long—but if you get there early, you may have a lucky chance. Only the Regulars are allowed special privileges. On rainy or hot days, they sit inside a small lobby until it is time to go on air. If they're late, they still get in anyhow—even when no one else can.

The WFIL studio is located in a section of West Philadelphia. Most of the Regulars take an el train, which stops right above Simon "Pop" Singer's luncheonette, where the stars of the show congregate before and after the live broadcast.

The establishment can be described as a glorified hole-in-the-wall consisting of four booths, a counter, a telephone booth, and a small candy counter, which is covered with photos of Regulars. The air is filled with a mixture of cigarette smoke and hair spray. Pop himself is sweet—if you tell him that you've never been on the show before and ask him to help get you in, he usually will.

After you visit Pop, you walk past a bar and a row of houses on the way to the studio. The producers separate everyone into boys' and girls' lines. Then they organize you by whether you have a letter of reservation or not.

Once chosen to be on *American Bandstand*, you are led by a Regular (Ed Kelly, Charlie Hibib, or sometimes Monte Montes) through a series of halls and into the studio. The door you enter from is in the back left portion of the studio. Most people have heard over and over again how small the studio is, but to see it in person will amaze you. It is *tiny*. There's no other word to use.

Another thing you won't expect to see is color. What you see at home on a television screen is gray, but in person, the walls are actually a bright blue. As you walk toward the front, you see the autograph table and then the bleachers to your left. To your right is the dance floor. You sit and wait for the show to begin. At this point, Dick Clark talks for a few seconds. He doesn't give a lot of directions; he just announces the day's guest. Then the show starts.

The first fast records at 3:30 p.m. and 4 p.m. are for couples only. The studio is a madhouse during records. Everyone crowds right up front to get in view of the cameras, especially the Regulars. For anyone who wonders what the chances are of a Regular asking a visitor to dance: unless you are close with a Regular, they are practically nonexistent.

It is the oddest feeling being on the other side of the camera. For instance, Clark has a microphone that can only be heard in the studio. He sometimes calls back couples, which explains why you may see kids stop dancing and move back. Clark doesn't know all the dancers as well as you may think; he sometimes refers to a Regular as "the girl in the blue dress."

Finally, when 4:50 p.m. rolls around, reservations are given out for the next week, and you can usually snag one. When leaving the studio, you go out behind the guest spot through a door leading directly to the parking lot.

Then, out the cigarettes come again. (I sometimes wonder how the Regulars can be on the show for so long without a smoke.) If you follow the crowd, it is back to Pop's again for another Coke, and then onto the el train home.

Arlene Sullivan swimming in a sea of fan mail.

Arlene's Diary

Chapter 5

With my mom and dad, brothers Eddie and Tommy, and sister Theresa, outside our house on Chester Avenue. My brother Tommy is hiding behind me.

My mom and I often read the fan magazines together.

A 1957 picture.

This is my little sister, Theresa.

Posing with Frankie's new album.

Brian Hyland and I at Notre Dame dance in Easton, PA.

I got as many as 500 fan letters a day.

Fans sent me a lot of stuffed animals. I gave them to the Children's Hospital in Philadelphia.

I tried to teach Dick how to do the stroll. Dancing was not his strong suit.

Kenny came by to pick me up after he had left the show.

Carole Higbee and I at Pop Singer's after the show.

The Diary of Arlene Sullivan

One day in the early fifties when I was about twelve or thirteen, I came home from school and my mom was sitting on the couch watching this new TV show called *Bandstand*. Its host was Philadelphia radio DJ Bob Horn. I walked passed the TV and as far as my mother was concerned I was an invisible ghost walking through air. She never took her eyes off the little TV screen. "What is this?" I asked, stopping to take a look. "It's a new teenage dance show," she answered, motioning for me to be quiet. I don't know how long it had been on, but my mom already knew the names of some of the kids dancing. I wasn't surprised that she was watching a dance show. My father and mother loved to dance. My dad was more into music and dance than into sports. He never watched sports on TV, so growing up I never saw any wrestling or boxing matches, baseball or football games in our house. We just didn't have any interest in them. I still don't. I'd rather watch dance.

So, one day I sat down next to my mom, and joined her in watching *Bandstand*. It didn't take me long to get into a routine of joining her every day to watch the show. We both had our favorites; Tom DeNoble and Jerry Blavat were mine. I don't remember who hers were. One day my girlfriend from down the block and I ran into Jerry on the street. We were beside ourselves, almost crazy. Like typical teenagers, we ran up to him and asked him for his autograph. He was so kind to us, he left us giddy. That cemented it—I was an ardent fan of the show. Like my mom, I learned everybody's names and whom they were dating or, at least, dancing with. My mother and I were finally sharing something together. It brought us a little closer.

We lived in a small row house in Southwest Philadelphia. And when I say small, I mean small. We had three bedrooms but only one bathroom. We had a porch but it was enclosed, that's where you entered the house. After the porch came a small living room that led to an equally small dining room. The kitchen was in the back, and that's where my mom spent most of her time. I give my mother a lot of credit because I don't know how she did it. She made us three meals a day in addition to all her other household chores. We never missed a breakfast, and she had lunch ready for us when we came home. I went to the Good Shepherd Grammar School, which was in a beautiful grey stone building. I loved that building and was so proud to go there; but I had to walk about ten blocks to get there. That was a lot for a little girl. I did it four times a day.

When I arrived at school, I always looked so clean and polished, because my mother starched my uniform blouse. It was so stiff that it would take about 15 minutes to put it on! My arms would just not go easily into the sleeves. My grandmother Bella was an excellent seamstress. She made my uniforms, as well as her daughters' wedding dresses, and her

Brian Hyland, Gene Kaye, Tommy DeNoble and I signing autographs in Easton, PA.

Al Tribviani and I after the show.

Jimmy Peatross and I.

Yes, that's me up against the wall.

grandchildren's christening dresses. She even made our Easter outfits.

My dad worked two jobs. When he wasn't working, he was home building things. He loved carpentry; it was his hobby, and he made incredible things for us. He made my first dollhouse, as well as a cradle for my doll. They were nice, but what I really wanted was a cowboy hat and a holster with cap guns. But it was the first cradle I ever had, and that was great. He made knickknack shelves for our house and several of the neighbors' houses. He was such a gentle man, a special man. I loved him deeply. He constantly told me I could be or do anything I wanted; I constantly didn't believe him. How sad is that? He never took a vacation, so we never did either. We didn't have much, but we had everything.

My mother had a hard time expressing love. Most of the time, you never knew how she felt or what she was thinking. The only way she showed her love to us, my brothers and sisters and me, was to do everything for us. I never understood how she could do so much—cooking, cleaning, washing, and ironing, all of it. I think more moms back then did more housework. They didn't have to go out and work. They devoted their lives to their households. My mom was one of six children, three sisters, two brothers, and her. When I get together with my family, we all tell the same stories about how our parents when they were young had to work hard to please our grandmother. Grandmom was always sewing. As I said, she made everyone's dresses and anything they needed. I really loved her and got to know her well. She died at 96. My mother passed before her; she was only 67. My dad too. He was 59. I never really knew my grandfather. He died when I was six, and I don't remember much about him. We were poor in many ways, but had a rich family life. My parents always put us first.

In 1950, we got our first television. There weren't many shows on yet, and when they went off the air, a test pattern or picture of a TV tower stayed up all night. I watched a lot of TV, especially movies from the 30s and 40s. In fact, before *Bandstand* came on the air, its time spot was dedicated to old movies, mostly dreary English films. My favorite actors were Lana Turner, John Garfield, James Cagney, and Susan Hayward. These people put me in a trance. I couldn't do anything but sit and watch when they were on. And I bounced back and forth between who I wanted to be. Sometimes I wanted to be the actress, and other times I wanted to be the actor. I guess you could say I was confused, but I wasn't aware of what the confusion was then. I just knew that I was different. And, sadly, I thought being

With Teddy Randazzo and his guitarist at the Brooklyn Paramount.
Steve Brandt took this picture of me in New York City.
Frani and I being silly, as we often were.
Carole Scaldeferri and I under the el outside the AB studio.

different meant something was wrong with me.

My parents had a cabinet with a radio and a 78 rpm record player. I used to play their big 78 records. They included records of Frank Sinatra, Doris Day, and Mario Lanza. I could listen to that music all day (I still can). Mario Lanza was my favorite. When I was eight, my mom took my brothers and me to see *The Student Prince*. She knew I liked Mario Lanza and this was a treat. I told her I wanted to run away to Hollywood to meet him. That's when she told me he grew up right there in South Philly. I was shocked. I asked my parents to take me to his old neighborhood. They laughed.

One Christmas my parents gave me my first record player; it was a small square-shaped unit. In those days 45s only cost 60 cents. They also bought me little carrying cases to store the 45s. Each case came with a paper index, and every time I bought a new record, I would carefully write the song titles and performers on the index. There were even corresponding numbers to stick on the record. Each box held 50 records. I kept them with me for the next 50 years, and finally gave them to my friend Jimmy DePre who was only eighteen years old but really understood and loved the music. My record player was on constantly; it seemed like it had a life of its own. Sometimes, if I fell in love with a song, I would play that record over and over again. I loved music. I guess it was just another escape. My songs wanted me to be happy.

Getting into *Bandstand*

One night, after I had become hooked on *Bandstand*, I went to a party at my neighbor's house. To my surprise, Justine Carrelli was there. Now, Justine was one of the stars of *Bandstand*. At that time, the show was the number one afternoon show in the Delaware Valley, so she was incredibly popular in Philadelphia. I couldn't believe she was at this party! I was so excited to meet her. It didn't take long for me to ask her how I could get on the show. What would I have to do? She was very kind and told me to meet her outside the studio the next day. She said she'd take me in. My day was complete, and tomorrow would be even better.

I showed up outside the studio at 46th and Market Streets early. I was anxious and couldn't wait to walk through that door. I joined the line along the wall, and waited and waited, then, finally, I saw Justine. My heart started beating so fast it sent blood racing through my body. She got closer and I stepped forward. I put my hand out. She did not see me! She walked passed me and went inside without ever looking back. Everything in me sunk. My shoulders went down, and I was almost in tears. This was not my day to get on *Bandstand*.

With John DeMarco.

Here I am posing in Bucks County, PA.

Gene Kaye brought Tom DeNoble and me to his show in Easton, PA.

John DeMarco and I in his house in Brooklyn.

More posing in Bucks County, PA.

In Cleveland ready to go home to Philadelphia with a new Sinatra LP.

Tommy DeNoble, Brian Hyland, and I making an appearance in Easton, PA.

But, as always, there were a lot of kids who did not make it in. One who didn't make it in was Pat Molittieri. We started talking about our disappointment, and before long we left and went over to Pop Singer's drugstore down the street. Pop Singer's was where most of the regulars from the show came after the show was over. It was almost empty when we walked in. We had a great time, and it was the start of our friendship. We took the bus home together that day.

On our bus was one of the most popular regulars on the show. Her name was Rosemary, but everyone knew her as "Little Ro." Of course, Pat and I told her that Justine had reneged on her promise to get us into the show, and left us standing outside on the street. "I can get you guys in," she said. "But you have to promise to do something for me." "Sure, anything," we said. We were willing to sell our teenage souls to get into *Bandstand*. Little Ro asked if we'd be willing to skip school the next day, and go with her to visit her boyfriend Nino, also a regular on the show. If we did, she said, she'd get us in that day. At first I thought it was a bad idea, and that I could get into trouble for skipping school. But it only took me two minutes to reconsider. I thought about my mom seeing me on TV. I said okay.

I met Little Ro the next morning at the subway, and together we went over to Nino's house. Nino was at work, so we spent the morning with his mother, a very lovely lady. Nino did a double take when he got home from work. He had broken up with Ro a week ago, and she was the last person he'd ever expect to see sitting in his living room. And with a stranger no less! Ro was devastated by the breakup and simply had to see him; but she didn't have the nerve to see him alone. She was really hurting. I felt bad for her, but to be honest all I could think about was getting into *Bandstand*. Little Ro's reunion wasn't working out very well, so we left Nino's house pretty quickly and headed over to the studio.

It was so exciting to walk through those doors with a Regular. I felt like someone on the inside. And I liked that feeling. I loved the feeling. Ro greeted everyone in sight and introduced me to everyone she said hello to. Everyone liked her. Part of me wanted to be like her, but I was so painfully shy I could hardly say hello back to anyone. As I stood there frozen, not knowing what to do, a boy named Sid Payne asked me to dance. "Oh my God," I said to myself. Someone asked me to dance. Sid was also a Regular, and a really nice boy, but viewers didn't know him that well. It was different in the studio; everyone knew him and loved him. He was one of the most popular guys with the Regulars. And he asked me to dance.

Ro threw a PJ party that weekend and invited me. Again, I couldn't believe it. I had known the girl one day and there I was, going to a party with all the other Regulars. By a fluke, I was suddenly in the in-crowd.

Getting My Card

After that first day, I kept coming back to the show. Then one day my friend got me a committee card, making me a Regular. Tony Mammarella, the executive producer, called me over and said, "Here's your card. You don't have to stand in line anymore. You come right in, every day." Despite being accepted, I was still shy. I was afraid to smile, as if that would break the spell. One day Dick took me aside and handed me a letter. "I have a letter for you, and they want to know all about you." Letters started pouring in. Dick started talking to me on the air. He would call me over, and say, "I'm going to talk to you after the commercial."

It wasn't long after that I became a regular dancer on the show. That meant I had to be there three or four times a week, which I had no problem with. My mother watched the show every day and saw me on it, but she never said much about it. It was as if I weren't on the show. I had gone to it for her, and it simply didn't matter. That's my mother and my disappointment. My dad objected too; but he knew it made me happy, so he said I could continue.

A lot of viewers started to write to Dick Clark about me and I started to receive fan letters. One popular Regular asked me, "Why are they writing to you? You haven't been here that long." "I don't know," I answered with a shrug. I was smiling on the inside. She was a friend, but sometimes even friends say mean things; nevertheless, I stayed loyal to her. It wasn't long after, I was getting more fan mail than she was. Ultimately I would get about 500 letters a week.

One day, not long after I started coming to the show, Dick took me aside and told me that a woman had sent in a blouse and skirt she had made for me. Dick asked me to wear it. "The woman will be thrilled to see you in it," he said. I told Dick I didn't think I could do it. I was devastated. I knew I was disappointing him. Then he said, "Actually, it's her nine-year-old son who likes you. He asked his mother to make this for you." I swallowed my pride and said okay, I will wear it; but I was still dying inside. The skirt and blouse were made

WFIL-TV
BANDSTAND CLUB
MEMBERSHIP CARD
ISSUED TO Arlene Sullivan
SUBJECT TO ALL CLUB RULES
GOOD ONLY
JAN., FEB., MAR., 1960
Dick Clark
Hon. Pres. Bandstand Club

My membership card.

of white satin with big black musical notes running through them. I did it, and after the show the little boy came in with his father. When I saw his face I knew I had done the right thing.

I had a lot of friends in the neighborhood that I hung out with, but to be honest, I loved being alone. On weekends, I would leave the house and go to the movies at the Benn or Benson Theater. They were only a dime in those days, and I could have stayed 'til midnight if I could have. I loved movies.

My Italian mom was obsessive about my brothers and me; well, she was obsessive about a lot of things. She never let us do chores around the house; they were strictly her domains. She spoiled us. To her, this was love. She was not affectionate. She didn't hug us; she almost never touched us. She just went about her way, making our lives comfortable. My father, on the other hand, was the opposite; he was very affectionate. He hugged us, kissed us, made things for us, and took us places around the city. He was what most people think of when they think of a good father. He was laid back, kind, and warm. I think my mom was jealous of him and of his relationships with us. But I'm speculating because I never understood my mother. She made me angry sometimes, and more than a little confused, because she never wanted to spend any time with me. She never took the time to teach me things. We never shared those special mother-daughter moments where you play with makeup and clothes and hair-dos. She never taught me how to be a "girly" girl. I had to watch her from afar as she applied her makeup and fixed her hair. I always told her how pretty she was, hoping that would melt her heart, make her reach out and take me in her arms and thank me. But that was just a dream, a dream that never happened. I loved her, but because those special moments never happened, I never knew who I was. I had no self-confidence.

Jamboree

Dick had just been cast in his first movie, *Jamboree*. To get some publicity for the film, he decided to hold a contest that would allow the viewers to choose four teenage girls to play autograph seekers for the movie's star. When the votes were counted, the four girls chosen were Justine, Rosalie, Dottie, and I. We were thrilled beyond belief. We went up to New York on a train with our moms. Unfortunately, we only got about a second and a half of screen time. Blink and you'll never see us. But it didn't matter, it was my first trip to New York City and that in itself was exciting.

Kenny Rossi

Occasionally I used to stand on the dance floor and look at the kids in the bleachers. One day, I noticed a guy with dark curly hair sitting alone in the third row. He was adorable, and he looked so shy. I think that shyness reminded me of myself. In an unexpected instant, our eyes met; I motioned to him to come down and dance with me. I had been on the show about a year by then, so I was somewhat known in the studio. Kenny came down immediately and we danced a slow dance. It didn't take much to know we clicked. I felt comfortable with him. He was respectful and gentle. We danced together the rest of the day. I asked him if he would be there the next day; he said he didn't know because he had just barely made the cut that day. I told him I'd meet him outside the next day and bring him in. I was there, and he showed up. I brought him in with me. We danced every dance together that day too. I introduced him around and soon viewers started noticing us. Suddenly *Bandstand* had another popular couple. Justine and Bob were the big stars then; they were blonds. Kenny and I were the new dark-haired couple.

Pop Singer, Kenny, and I outside Pop's store.

We always danced together, unless, of course, as often happens with teenagers, we had an argument. On those days, we danced with other people. This upset so many fans. We heard from a lot of them. One person sent a telegram (long before the internet or mobile phones). Dick Clark read it on the air. It read, "Kenny, don't cut off your nose to spite your face." The fans were blaming Kenny for the argument. But it wasn't he, it was I! I felt terrible. Dick called us down to the dance floor and made us the featured couple.

Kenny was the kind of kid any parent would be glad to let into their home or date their daughter. Kenny and I had what you can call a "puppy love"romance. It was the fifties, and on the surface everything was innocent. Most kids were not having sex. We would steam the windows of the car and think we were risqué. Kids today are so much more advanced, not really mature, but advanced when it comes to sexual things. We were not. I'm beginning to sound like my mother! It was a great time to grow up. Other than the atom bomb, we didn't have a lot to fear. I danced on *American Bandstand* five days a week after school. Some parents objected to the show and forbade their kids from going on, but when they ultimately saw that the boys had to wear suits and ties and the girls had to dress modestly (nothing tight), they began to lighten up. Besides, they knew where their kids were and what they were doing. If there were a show like *American Bandstand* today, I'm sure parents would be counting their blessings.

Kenny and I on a photo shoot in New York City's Central Park.

The boys on the show took a lot of bullying from Philadelphia boys, almost never from guys outside the city. One night, Kenny and I were coming home from visiting a friend in North Philadelphia. We were crossing the street to catch the el. There was a car sitting at a red light. Spotting us, someone in the car yelled, "Hey, Bandstand!" We kept walking. Then we heard the car doors slam. All of a sudden there were three boys coming after us. They got Kenny up the steps of the el and started hitting him. I was pounding one of them with my handbag. I hit one guy's glasses. I wanted to throw those glasses into the street, but I didn't. I shouted, "Leave him alone! Leave him alone!" Kenny jumped the turnstile and got away from them. It was horrifying, but some of the guys faced that kind of bullying every day.

Kenny and I and a couple of other regulars took a trip one Saturday afternoon up to New York. We were going to the Little Theater off Broadway on 44th Street; Dick Clark originated his Saturday Night show from the theater. We hadn't been there since Dick had brought us up on a bus to appear on his first show. It was a night we will never forget. Dick wanted all of us in the audience that night. He hired a bus to take us to New York. My mother was one of the chaperones. When the bus pulled up in front of the theater, to our amazement, there were hundreds of kids screaming and yelling. They were there to see us. There were police barricades and mounted policemen.

We weren't allowed off the bus until the police escorted us off. When I finally left the bus, I had a cop on each arm. Still, someone grabbed my hair and started pulling it. That was the first time I realized how big *American Bandstand* was—and how big *we* were. It was crazy, mayhem. I had never experienced that before, none of us had. After the show, it was the same tumultuous scene. Once again the police took us one-by-one back to the bus, but our departure was delayed; the police discovered two girls had locked themselves into the bathroom on the bus. Now that's dedication!

A while after that first trip to the show, a couple of us went up to the show on our own. We took the train from Philadelphia and decided to walk to the theater. When we started up 44th Street, someone shouted, "It's Kenny and Arlene!" In a flash, kids who had been standing in line rushed us. It was a stampede; the crowd separated Kenny and me. I didn't know what to do. I was petrified. They were pulling at my clothes. I began to run. A policeman crashed through the crowd and grabbed me before I got very far. He took me across the street to the Hotel Astor and told me to sit quietly in the lobby. I told him they had taken after Kenny, chasing him down the street. I didn't know where he was. The kids were screaming and laughing, but it wasn't funny. When he found Kenny, a crowd of girls had surrounded him tearing at his clothes and hair. It was like a scene out of *The Birds*. The policeman brought Kenny back to the hotel and told us to grab our things, get our friends, and go home to Philadelphia. We were happy to oblige.

Kenny and I each won one of these funny Italian cars, the Isetta 300. It had three wheels and opened in the front. A lot of police departments use cars like this for traffic control.

Winning the Car

Every year on *American Bandstand* Dick had a dance contest. In 1957, it was a jitterbug contest. Almost three quarters of a million votes came in. Justine and Bob were the big winners. They were the most popular couple on the show, so it was no surprise that they won—the contest, after all, was really just a popularity contest. They each won a jukebox filled with records. Once you won a contest, you could not compete in another. In 1958, Kenny and I won first place in the Cha Cha contest. We each won an Isetta 300, a peculiar Italian car with three wheels that opened in the front. Kenny's car was green and mine was blue. We were only fifteen, so we couldn't drive them. Kenny's brother drove us around town in Kenny's car. I don't know whatever happened to his car after he left *Bandstand* and started his singing career. I told my parents they could sell mine and keep the money. I told them to buy my sister Theresa a bike, something I always wanted, but never had. Pat Molittieri won an in-ground swimming pool for her win, and Frani Giordano and Mike Balara took home 1961 Ford convertibles for winning the Pony Contest. In 1961, Jimmy Peatross and Joan Buck won a slow dance contest. They won because they were good. They were the best. They also won cars.

That I wanted a bike was no secret; my friend's mother knew I wanted one, so she let me borrow her daughter's bike whenever I wanted. Her daughter didn't use her bike often. I would go over to their house early in the morning, get the bike, and ride from neighborhood to neighborhood all day. My friend was an only child and never minded sharing. She and her family were so kind to me. I loved them, and when I was on that bike, I felt free and so happy. I always brought the bike back around four in the afternoon, because I had to be home for dinner by five. The whole family had to be there at that table; it was a rule in our house. My mom never missed a meal. During the week, it was always a big meal. On Tuesdays, Thursdays, and Sundays we had pasta. She was Italian, and this was her specialty. And the pasta dishes varied, sometimes with meatballs and sausages, other times with chicken or veal cutlets. They were all so delicious. She was such a good cook. She cooked for us every night but Saturday, her break night, as she called it. That was the night we had pizza or sandwiches. When I think back, I'm amazed at how hard she worked in that kitchen; it was a real labor of love.

When Kenny left the show he recorded a few records and toured the country. He even made a few appearances on *American Bandstand*. I was already gone by that time, so I didn't get to see him. We went our separate ways. He got married, had a baby girl. Unfortunately, that marriage didn't work and he raised his little girl as a single dad. He did a great job because his daughter is wonderful today. He remarried and had a second child, a boy. It all worked out for him. Today, he runs his own business outside of Philadelphia and is doing well. He will always have a special place in my heart, and in my life.

Barbara Levick

Barbara Levick, a regular from *American Bandstand*, and I went to Texas to visit a friend of hers who lived in Ft. Worth. I'd never been to the South or West before, and it was eye-opening. Barbara's friend was a teenage girl who lived with her mother and grandmother. They were so nice to us, but one day a group of teenage girls of Mexican descent heard we were in the neighborhood. They came knocking on the front door to see us. The grandmother answered the door. She called us to the door, then told the girls to get off her front steps. Barbara and I went outside to talk to the girls, who at this point were bubbly and excited to meet us—they watched *American Bandstand* too. The grandmother came outside and ordered the girls off the sidewalk. "If you want to talk to them," she said, angrily, "you have to talk to them in the street." The girls, obviously used to this kind of intolerance, started to walk away. I stopped them, and told them if they wanted to talk to us, it would be right there on the sidewalk. The grandmother was fuming, and went into the house, slamming the front door. Barbara and I had a wonderful time with these girls. Rather than go back into the house, Barbara and I took a bus downtown. We wanted to see the city.

When I got on the bus, I immediately went to the back. In Philly, I always rode in the back of the bus or trolley. I was very comfortable there. Suddenly, everyone on the bus was telling me to come up front. Barbara told me only "colored" people rode back there! I didn't give a damn. I wanted to sit there, not in the front. I was a kind-of white Rosa Parks in reverse. The sad part was that this was the first time I had actually felt the racial tension that was so prevalent in the country then. Philadelphia was a de facto segregated city. There were no blacks near my

Frani and I with Angela South, a fan from Atlanta.

Carmen, Jay, and I after the show.

Dancing with Tony Porrini.

Joe Wissert, Frankie Lobis, friends, and I at the Latin Casino to see Sammy Davis Jr.

Frankie Lobis and I at the Latin Casino to see Johnny Mathis.

Frankie Lobis and I on our way to see Oprah in Chicago.

Carmen and I clubbing after the Oprah show.

Spending an early morning at the *Today Show* with Matt Lauer, Vicki, and Ann Curry (thanks to Ray Smith).

I'm with Bobby Vee at the opening of Dick Clark's theater in Branson, MO.

Sitting with Glenn Campbell at the 33 1/3 reunion.

Fats Domino playing the piano for me in New Orleans only hours before Hurricane Katrina destroyed his house.

Lucie Arnaz sat down and schmoozed with me for a moment at Birdland.

neighborhood, and few in the schools I went to. There were no blacks on *Bandstand*, even though the studio was in a mixed neighborhood. But this was different. This was dangerous, and mean. I told Barbara it was time to go home; I didn't like these people.

Judy Hill

The trip to Texas did not go well, but I had become friends with a girl named Judy Hill there. After an argument with Barbara, I asked if I could stay with Judy's family. Judy's mom called my mother and asked if it would be okay for me to stay with them. My mother said no. She told me to come home. Mrs. Hill calmed my mother, and she finally said I could stay. A couple days later, Barbara came and stayed with the Hills too.

Judy and I became friends and her parents brought her to Philly to see me. They stayed in a hotel, and came to our house for a big Italian dinner. They were floored. It was a whole different world for them, coming to a row house. She came to the show with me and had a great time. She met everyone. She was a beautiful girl.

In the 60s we corresponded for a while but as often happens, we lost touch. She got married, I know that. Then one day, I was watching *The Phil Donahue Show*. He was interviewing Martina Navratilova's ex-lover who was suing Martina for palimony. The woman's name was Judy Nelson. She mentioned she was from Ft. Worth and had written a book. I ran out and got the book. Her maiden name was Judy Hill.

I called the publishing company and said I was an old friend. I told them I didn't know if she would remember me, but "Please tell her to call Arlene Sullivan." She called the next day. She asked me what I had been up to. I told her that when I turned 18, I realized I was a lesbian. She was hysterical; we had something in common. She came to Philadelphia and we got together. In fact, we went to a Joni Mitchell concert. She was living in Virginia on a horse farm near the University of Virginia at the time and she invited me to come visit. It is just such a small world, and a strange world, sometimes.

Meeting Steve Brandt

One day on the show, a young man, who was a few years older than most of us, came up to me and said he thought the regulars should be featured in some teen magazines. He said we were very popular and other kids would love to read about us. His name was Steve Brandt and he was from Brooklyn with a heavy Brooklyn accent. His accent seemed so out of place in Philly, where we had an equally strong accent. He asked if I could get some of the regulars together and meet him that evening in Rittenhouse Square in Center City. The square is in a very tony section of the city and was known as a gay meeting place in the city. We were thrilled to meet him. Everyone liked Steve and in no time he was one of us. We started to hang out at Rittenhouse Square. The girls on the show were very accepting of the gay guys.

Steve Brandt and I.

After Kenny left the show, I danced with Jimmy Peatross most of the time. Jimmy and his usual partner Joan Buck were probably the best dancers that were ever on the show. When you danced with Jimmy, he made you feel like Ginger Rogers. He was so good. Well, Jimmy and a few of the other guys on the show used to hang out in Rittenhouse Square. In the sixties, this little park became our home away from home. This is where I met the gay community, the community that I would soon be calling my family. I knew I was different early on, but being with all these friends, I came to terms with my feelings. "I kissed a girl, and I liked it!" I was in various relationships with women, and was happy to have found my way so early. Growing up in the city and socializing with my friends from *Bandstand* gave me strength to follow my feelings. But being gay in the fifties and sixties was not a gay old time. It was a struggle. The public looked down on us, and a lot of us looked down on ourselves. I am so happy for the kids today, that, although it may still be tough to be out, it doesn't carry the same stigmas.

It was during that time that I discovered some of the girls on the show were also gay. I was just totally confused by then. And as I said before, I started to dismiss my feelings for other girls. Steve lived in New York, but was spending a lot of time in Philadelphia. He and I became very close, and he would come over to my house for dinner every time he was in the city. My family really enjoyed him. Steve was a bit feminine, and my mom would roar with laughter every time he imitated Marilyn Monroe.

If you were a regular on *American Bandstand* and you turned seventeen, your time was up; gone overnight were all your privileges. You could no longer buck the lines outside and go into the studio. You were forced to leave the fantasy world of television, and enter the real world of work. Although I wasn't working for it, *16 Magazine* would periodically send me small checks for letting them feature me; some of the articles even carried my name as writer. I would also do some appearances for the magazine. Once, they sent me to the Brooklyn Paramount for an Alan Freed Rock 'n' Roll show. Bobby Rydell, Jackie Wilson, and Teddy Randazzo were three of the headliners. Alan asked me to introduce Bobby; it was an extraordinary moment. I never thought when I started dancing on *Bandstand* that I would experience moments like that.

After my stint at *16 Magazine* ended, I had to find a real job. I took some typing courses and then took some office jobs. One of those jobs was at Dun & Bradstreet. Before long I started working in the hotel business. I booked meetings, benefits, various events. Once I booked a seminar with Dick Clark. The room was filled with DJs from across the country. Dick took a

Ro

One of the things that always puzzled me was how viewers learned my home address. Because they did, some would end up waiting outside my house for me; or sometimes, they would be waiting for me in my living room. My mom let them in. One Saturday morning, my mom woke me to let me know that there were some kids from the Bronx downstairs waiting for me. My mother almost always let strangers in; she often fed them too. I jumped out of bed that morning, dressed, fixed my hair, and headed downstairs. One of the girls, Ro, told me she thought we looked alike. She was beautiful, so I agreed with her. She and I became friends and managed to get together over the years. I remember visiting her and her brother in the Bronx. In the seventies, we met in Provincetown. She was with a woman partner. We did a lot of laughing and reminiscing that week.

A few weeks ago, Ro's brother Vinny called me and invited me to a surprise 75th birthday party for Ro on City Island (part of the Bronx). He told his sister that I was the first girl he ever kissed. She told him I was the first girl she ever kissed. I don't remember kissing him, but who knows. It was a night full of memories and laughter.

Another time, a young girl from Cleveland was waiting on my porch for me. My mother told me she had run away from home. I looked at her and couldn't believe she had come all the way to Philly by herself. While we talked, my mother called her parents and told them she was safe. They said they would come to Philadelphia to pick her up. She said she was my #1 fan. I told her I would keep in touch and did so for many years. The last time we spoke she was living with a woman in San Francisco. The thing about the gay community in those days was how easy it was to run into each other. One night I met three guys in a gay club; they were from the street that I grew up on. And there was the woman who lived around the corner from me—turns out she was a gay councilwoman in Philly.

Paul Anka and I at Scioli's in Philadelphia.

Paul and I in Washington, DC. He was appearing with Annette; I was staying with Annette and her family.

Paul Anka and I took a photo with a fan. We didn't have selfies then.

Paul Anka

When Paul Anka first appeared on *American Bandstand*, he asked the producer Tony Mammarella if he could meet me. Tony came over to me and told me Paul had asked to meet me. Oh my God, my heart started pounding. Paul Anka was one of my fantasies. I loved his record "Diana." I didn't have a clue why he asked to see me. When we met, he told me that every time Dick played "Diana," he noticed I would light up and smile. He said I looked like I loved dancing to his song. I did. He also told me I was his sister's favorite Regular. He asked if I would call her. I did, and, as often happened, Marion and I became friends. She invited me to the family's house in North Jersey. My parents said okay and my father drove me up. I spent the weekend with Marion, her little brother, and their parents. Paul lived in his own place on the property. One night he took all of us to Palisades Amusement Park. What a thrill that was. Marion came to the show a few times in Philadelphia.

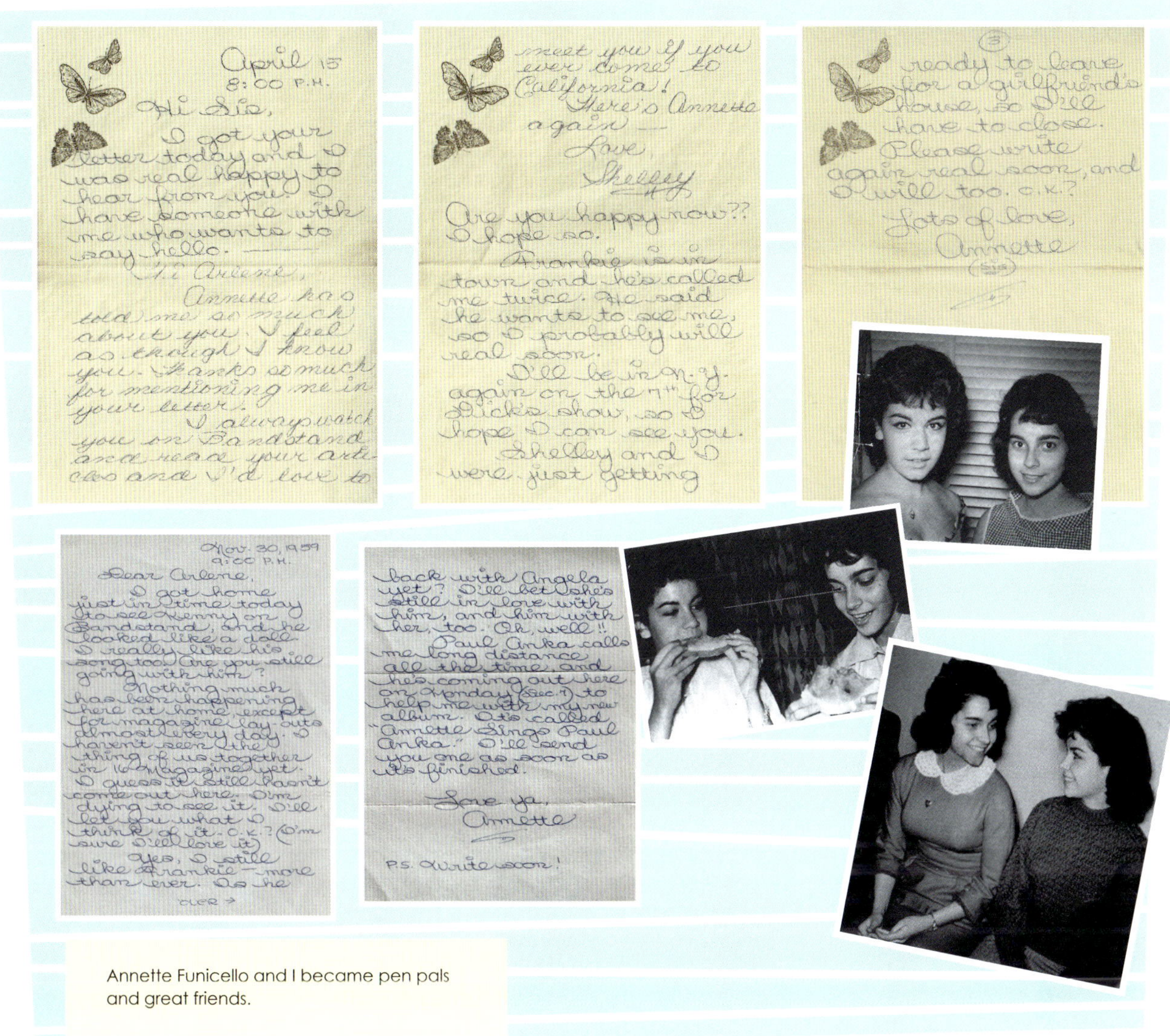

April 15
8:00 P.M.
Hi Sis,
I got your letter today and I was real happy to hear from you. I have someone with me who wants to say hello. ——
Hi Arlene,
Annette has told me so much about you. I feel as though I know you. Thanks so much for mentioning me in your letter.
I always watch you on Bandstand and read your articles and I'd love to meet you if you ever come to California!
There's Annette again —
Love,
Shelley
Are you happy now?? I hope so.
Frankie is in town and he's called me twice. He said he wants to see me, so I probably will real soon.
I'll be in N.Y. again on the 7th for Dick's show, so I hope I can see you.
Shelley and I were just getting

(3)
ready to leave for a girlfriend's house, so I'll have to close. Please write again real soon, and I will too. O.K.?
Lots of love,
Annette
(Sis)

Nov. 30, 1959
9:00 P.M.
Dear Arlene,
I got home just in time today to see Kenny on Bandstand, and he looked like a doll. I really like his song too. Are you still going with him?
Nothing much has been happening here at home, except for magazine lay-outs almost every day. I haven't seen the thing of us together in 16 Magazine yet. I guess it still hasn't come out here. I'm dying to see it. I'll let you what I think of it. O.K.? (I'm sure I'll love it)
Yes, I still like Frankie — more than ever. Is he
over →

back with Angela yet? I'll bet she's still in love with him, and him with her, too. Oh, well!!
Paul Anka calls me long distance all the time, and he's coming out here on Monday (Dec. 7) to help me with my new album. It's called "Annette Sings Paul Anka." I'll send you one as soon as it's finished.
Love ya,
Annette
P.S. Write soon!

Annette Funicello and I became pen pals and great friends.

Annette

When Annette Funicello appeared on the show, she came up to me and told me how many people she met told her we look alike. I said I also get a lot of letters comparing us. I was flattered. She asked if we could exchange addresses. We did, and we became friends and even thought of each other as sisters. She was one of the nicest girls I had ever met. She was as beautiful on the inside as she was on the outside. When she was appearing at various venues on the East Coast, her mother would call my mom and ask if I could spend time with Annette. I would meet her at Radio City Music Hall in New York City, or some theater in Washington D.C. Her parents would make all the arrangements, and handle all the expenses. They were so generous. They made sure I was safe, and had cars pick me up and bring me home. Her mother was so glad she had someone to hang out with in the down times, someone who was her own age (she was born in October 1942, I was born in November). We had so many good times together. As often happens, we lost touch over the years, but I always stayed up-to-date with her career, her family, and, unfortunately, her health problems. My memories of Annette are always with me.

Charlie Gracie and I in front of the *Bandstand* mural in the old *Bandstand* studio.
Dion and I backstage at the Hilton in Atlantic City.
With Dion; his manager, Dick Fox; and Dion's wife, Susan.
Fabian and I at a rehearsal for the reunion show.

Dion

One night, Annette invited me to her sixteenth birthday party at a hotel in New York City. I met Susan that night, Dion DeMucci's girlfriend. The three of us hit it off and we had a whole night of laughing and silliness. I saw Susan a few years ago when Dion was appearing at Caesar's Palace in Atlantic City. I was invited to go backstage and say hi; Dion doesn't usually let people come backstage, so I felt privileged. Dion and Susan are one of the nicest couples in the business, and Dion is as good, if not better, as he was back in the day. His voice and presence on stage is still strong and captivating. One time while working with *16 Magazine* I met Dion's sister Donna. She invited me to spend a weekend with her and the family in White Plains, New York. I was great to be there because they treated me like family. We made a lovely family.

Danny & the Juniors

Of all the people who appeared on *American Bandstand*, I had my biggest crush on Danny Rapp, the Danny of Danny and the Juniors. Danny and all the juniors were from my neighborhood in Southwest Philadelphia. I identified with them. Danny had many girlfriends at the time; the band members were so young and so busy they really couldn't get serious with any one girl. Danny Rapp was my first heartbreaker.

Bobby Darin

Bobby appeared on *Bandstand* when he was promoting his record "I Found A Million Dollar Baby (in a Five and Ten Cent Store)." He was so talented, and when he was on the show, he was so confident. He had that "it" factor. He told us he was going to be doing a show down in Wildwood, New Jersey, and that we should come see him. A group of us went down the shore one weekend and got to hang out with him before his show. What a great personality.

Charlie Gracie

I met Charlie Gracie on *Bandstand* when the show was still local. He was a talented guy from South Philadelphia and at the time had a giant hit called "Butterfly." The record sold a phenomenal three million copies. That was a lot for a rock 'n' roll record. In fact, he helped put rock 'n' roll on the map. Despite his success, he was always kind and great with his fans. My girlfriend Ro and I were super fans, and one time we were at his parents' house when he returned from a gig in London. Dick Clark and Charlie had a stormy, bitter relationship over money that cost Charlie his career in the states. But Europe, and especially Great Britain, loved him and kept his career alive. Ro and I started a Charlie Gracie fan club.

Charlie is still performing today, and has written

Jerry Blavat with his ever-present baseball cap.
Jerry Blavat letting me have a few words on his radio show.
I'm with Jerry Blavat a lot.
Eddie Kelly, Frankie Avalon, Frankie Lobis, and I in LA.
Carmen, Bobby Rydell, and I in Los Angeles.

an autobiography called *Rock & Roll's Hidden Giant*. So many rock greats (Paul McCartney, Graham Nash, etc.) cite Charlie as one of the major influences on their careers. I run into him from time to time, at parties and shows, and no matter what the venue, he is always convivial and gracious. He has not changed in all these years; he still appreciates his fans. What a great guy. I'm so proud to be able to call him a friend.

Jerry Blavat

Before I ever went to *Bandstand*, I watched the show at home every day, long before Dick Clark took over. The host in the early days was Bob Horn. I knew the names of all the regulars. My favorite was Jerry Blavat. He stood out to me. He was the most popular guy at the time. Over the years, he and I have become good friends. He is a well-known DJ in this area, and today at 76, he moves and acts as vibrantly as he did back in the early fifties. Jerry still plays "our" music from the fifties and sixties. He runs dances all over New Jersey and Delaware County in Pennsylvania. I try to go to his radio show and dance every week at the Golden Nugget. Jerry Blavat keeps us moving, and dancing keeps me smiling. I love it. He has a compelling autobiography out called *You Only Rock Once*. Thank you, Jerry Blavat!

Bobby Rydell

One day after arriving at the studio, Carole Gibson ran up to me and told me that her old boyfriend Bobby Rydell was going to be a guest on the show that day. She was so excited for him and wanted me to meet him. When he arrived, he saw Carole and immediately came over and gave her a big hug. She quickly introduced me and once again I swooned. He was like a breath of fresh air in the studio. Like the other South Philadelphia boy singers, Bobby was exceedingly polite. Carole said that when Dick introduced Bobby we had to scream, and scream loud. But Bobby is so talented, we would have screamed anyway. I could see how he and Carole could have been attracted to each other. Bobby never left the Philadelphia area, even after hitting it big in *Bye, Bye Birdie*. Consequently, I see him around often and I can tell you he is as kind and as much fun today as he was back in the fifties. He, too, has an autobiography out. It's called *Bobby Rydell: Teen Idol on the Rocks*.

Fabian

There weren't many people in the fifties who did not think that Fabian was the handsomest boy they'd ever seen. He was stunning. Beautiful, if you will. He was in my friend Carole Gibson's class, and she had a major

Frankie Avalon and I.
Frankie signing books for me and Ray Smith.
Frankie Avalon, Ray Smith, and I in Atlantic City after Frankie's show.
Here I am with Ray Smith.
Ray and I trying to raise a little cash doing the jitterbug in front of the Eiffel Tower in Paris.

crush on him. "Let's call him," she said one day. "Let's see if he'll meet us somewhere." To our amazement, he agreed. We were beaming when we left Carole's house; we were proverbial schoolgirls rushing and giggling to meet a boy. We headed to the street corner four blocks away where we had told him to meet us. We laughed all the way over. I had never seen this so-called beauty, so I was curious. We turned the corner and BAM! There he was standing against the wall waiting for us. "Oh, my God," I said to myself. He was everything Carole said he was. With his big white teeth, thick dark eyebrows, and green eyes, I was staring and swooning. Carole introduced me and for a moment all my words caught in my throat. I shook his hand and meekly said, "Hi." I was shocked that he was shy. He was gentle and sweet, but surprisingly shy. How can anyone who looks like that be shy? He told us that he watched us all the time on *American Bandstand*. I was thrilled. We stood on that corner for about an hour talking and laughing.

The next time I saw Fabian, I was at a dance in Easton, Pennsylvania. The DJ Gene Kaye invited me to the dance at Notre Dame as a guest. He had musical guests at all his dances. I guess I qualified because I danced. It was the most popular dance in that region and I was happy to be there. I was also happy because I was with my good friend Annette Funicello. While Annette was on stage lip-syncing her latest record, I was standing in the wings watching. Suddenly, I looked behind me, and standing there was Fabian. He hadn't yet released any records, so I asked him what he was doing there. "I just cut a record," he whispered, "and I'm going to perform it for the first time tonight." He was nervous, but once he got on stage the place erupted with cheers and screams and he seemed a bit more comfortable. I was so happy for him. He went on to have a nice career, most of it though on the big screen. He made a slew of movies, many with the biggest stars of the era (Jimmy Stewart, John Wayne, Peter Lorre, Henry Fonda, Tab Hunter). I run into him from time to time and we always laugh about the "old" days.

Frankie Avalon

I met Frankie Avalon on *American Bandstand*. He was singing one day and I was sitting on the bleachers studying his face. He was so Italian—dark hair and sunny smile. He could have been part of my family. He had an easy way about him. The girls at the show loved him from the first time they saw him in person.

I, too, fell under his spell. In 1958, he invited me to his eighteenth birthday party at Palumbo's Supper Club in South Philadelphia. Frankie had appeared there many times (actually at an extension of the club called the CR Room). He played the trumpet. I was going to his party with my friend Carole Gibson. One of the reasons I remember the party so well is when Carole walked into the room, we did double takes. We were wearing the same dress. It was classic comedy right out of the movies. We laughed out loud. Our focus that night, however, was on Frankie, not our dresses. He was so gracious and generous to us, a real gentleman even at 18. Frankie is still performing and has a great Italian cookbook along with some delicious food products. After all these years, I still adore Frankie Avalon.

Ray Smith

In July 1997, I got a call from the people at Dick Clark Productions telling me that they had set up an interview for Dick's newest book on *Bandstand* with a guy named Ray Smith. That was fine with me. Ray called a few days later and we set up a time to meet at my apartment in New Jersey. He sounded friendly and professional. When he rang my doorbell, I remember opening the door and being knocked out by his broad friendly smile and bright attitude. He walked into the room as if he had been there many times before. We sat at the table and he turned on his tape recorder and we began. The first thing he told me was that he and I had been in the same homeroom at Bartram High School. We soon discovered that we were from the same neighborhood, went to the same dances, including *American Bandstand*, and knew many of the same people. How could it be that we had never met, especially since he had been on the show while I was there. Fate is funny in that way.

With all that information, I told him to turn off the tape machine, so that we could gossip. He told me he was gay. Apparently, the fact that I was came as a big shock. We left the apartment, went to lunch, and laughed for about six hours. I know that I say this a lot, but I loved him instantly, and he has never done anything to make me regret that. We are best friends today and one of the people I love to dance with. He tries to get down to the Jersey Shore often. He used to come all the time, but his house was destroyed in Super Storm Sandy. When Ray comes down, we make it over to Jerry Blavat's show or to his club Memories in Margate and dance. Ray lives in New York City, and I try to get up there to hang out with him as much as I can. We always have a good time, always. I am so glad he wandered into my life because he makes me happy, and because it was he who showed me one of my favorite places in the world—Paris. I love him.

Carol

I was still living at home in my twenties. No one seemed to mind it; certainly my parents didn't. My sister was eight years younger than I, and my brother eleven years younger. We were all living under one roof. The family moved out of the city to the suburbs. We moved to Bucks County about 20 miles from Philadelphia. This was difficult for my little sister. It's not easy leaving your friends and school chums at that age. But she adapted. I continued to work in the city and to hang out there every weekend.

One Saturday night I drove into the city and went to a popular club called the Mystic. The club had a mixed crowd and, unlike many people, I never minded going in alone. I knew the owners, so I was never really alone. Besides, I knew I'd run into some of my *Bandstand* buddies, as well as some gay friends I had met along the way. The club was a three-story affair with a piano bar on the first floor, a dance floor with a great jukebox on the second floor (for the most part, we didn't have DJs in those days), and an elegant restaurant on the third floor. I loved this club because it was totally mixed—gay, straight, men, women, young, and old.

On this particular Saturday night, I spotted a woman I had never seen there before. She was what you would call petite. She was adorable. I couldn't take my eyes off her. A friend saw me standing there staring at the dance floor; she came over and asked

Carol Galin and I in the 1980s.

Bandstand regular Joanne MonteCarlo and Vicki in Atlantic City.

I'm with Rocco Fiorentino, a twelve-year-old blind musical prodigy. We're at Birdland in New York City where he just performed.

Here I am with Walt Grzelak and his son at Egypt, a club in Philadelphia. We were celebrating the dedication of the *American Bandstand* Studios in 1997.

what I was doing. I told her I was smitten with a woman dancing on the other side of the room. She looked around the dance floor, and abruptly walked away. Two seconds later she appears with the girl on her arm. She introduces her to me. "Arlene, this is Carol. She's from New York City," she said, smiling. We exchanged some pleasantries. I was shaking inside. I think my hands were shaking too. "Wanna dance?" Carol asked. "Sure," I said with a big grin on my face. We walked onto the dance floor and were together for the next twelve years. Carol was my first live-in partner and it was a good twelve years. Although we have been separated for many years, we still talk on the phone every day. We are, more or less, sisters. Carol retired from teaching and is living with her partner of twenty-five years. Her partner is also my friend; it's nice how that happens. She'll always be a part of my life.

Colleen

When I started my career in the 1980s as a blackjack dealer at the casinos in Atlantic City, I met Colleen. We had a whirlwind romance, and made it last for nine years. Our breakup was devastating for both of us. I came to the conclusion that when it happens, "you break down, go off the deep end, but then, for your sanity, pick yourself up, and start all over again." It's a cliché but it works.

Vicki

In the 90s, I met this vivacious blonde athlete, Vicki. What a beauty, both inside and out, but it soon became clear that we were from two different worlds. She was a small town girl from a northwestern New Jersey town with fewer than 3,000 inhabitants. I, of course, was a city girl, born and bred. After ten years as partners, we decided it wasn't really meant to be. Today, we live as roommates and friends. We share our lives and it is working out beautifully.

The Other

My friend Larry Giuliani called me and asked me if I was going to go to the *Bandstand* reunion at Dick's new restaurant, the "Bandstand Grill," in King of Prussia. If I said yes, he would go too. It was quite a drive from my home in Ventnor, New Jersey, but I decided to make the trip. I am so glad I said yes. So is Larry. To my surprise, everybody was there. It was quite a turnout. Kenny Rossi brought his whole family—and I am always glad to see them. I hadn't seen a lot of the Regulars in a long time. One of them I hadn't seen since 1962. When she left the show, she married, had children, and did well. Her children were with her that night, though I never met them.

As I was standing on the side watching the dancers, she came over to me and told me how glad she was to see me after so many years. I felt the same. She was as attractive as she was those many years ago. Some people are like that, they don't lose their looks. It was no secret by then that I was gay. We found a table, sat down, and had a surprising conversation. She told me she was leading a double life. My eyes widened in disbelief. I leaned in to make sure I heard

With Vicki on summer vacation.

Vicki Cole and I on vacation in the 1990s.

After a dance extravaganza at a fancy private club in New York, I sat down with choreographer Johnnie Paolillo.

Sailing around Manhattan.

everything correctly. I formed the words in my mouth and told her I was a lesbian. What a moment. At least for me. We began talking to each other almost daily. Something was happening. "Would you like to take a weekend trip?" she asked, one night. "Yes," I said, acknowledging my feelings for her. So off we went. It was the beginning of an affair that never developed into anything more. Her life was complicated; she had a husband, children, and a woman on the side. And then there was me. That made me cautious and, to be honest, a little bit scared. I didn't understand how someone could juggle so many balls in the air. That's not easy and can never be fulfilling. It's not a recipe for happiness. I wanted to be happy, and so I kept a little distance.

During this time I started having heart problems, of all sorts. In one way my heart was breaking, in another, more serious way, it was beginning to fail me. Not long after, I had triple bypass surgery. I was sick, really sick, so I couldn't concentrate on her. I had to concentrate on me, and getting better. After a year of balancing her several lives, and my inattention, she decided to leave her husband, stay with her female friend, and say goodbye to me. It was sad. But again, I learned that when these difficult things weigh you down, you simply have to pick yourself up, dust yourself off, and start all over again.

I went to a state fair in Detroit one time with a friend. Dick Clark had a rock 'n' roll show there—we didn't know that at the time. One of the singers in the show Freddy Cannon ("Tallahassee Lassie") spotted me and asked Dick to put a couple of chairs out front for us. When we walked out, the crowd went crazy. Dick looked at us and said, "Oh yeah, I forgot they know who you are."

A few years ago at a fancy party on Fifth Avenue in New York, a man in a tux in his late sixties came over and told me he grew up on a ranch in Wyoming. He said when he was a kid, he would come in off the range every day to watch me on *Bandstand*. He said, "In all my days, I never thought that I would ever meet you, and here you are standing right in front of me." That was an emotional moment for both of us.

Today

I have to say I am so blessed to have such great friends and family. Ray showed me Paris, and my cousins Ken and Mary took me to Italy where they introduced me to part of my heritage. I love them all. It's Thanksgiving Day today and I am home with the flu. It's unusually warm for this time of year, so I am sitting out on my balcony basking in the unexpected spring-like weather. If I sit real still, I can hear the most comforting quiet in the world. No cars, no people yelling, only the sounds of water and birds. A passing boat on the bay below looks as if it is sailing on a sea of glass. The water is calm and mesmerizing. I feel at peace today (except for an occasional sneeze and clogged nose). I love my home. Home is a simple pleasure.

My Grandmother's Smiling

By Joe Marrella

Watching *American Bandstand* was part of my Grandmother's routine every day. She loved to watch the couples, follow their lives, and select her favorites. For whatever reason, Arlene Sullivan was her favorite. So much so that all I heard from her again and again was, "Joseph, please ask her to dance when you go to the show, I love Arlene."

Of course, I tried to explain to her that Arlene was going with Kenny; hence the phrase repeated hundreds of times on the show, "Here's Arlene & Kenny"—a phrase even mentioned years later in the movie *Peggy Sue Got Married*.

Well, when your grandmother asks you to do something, especially something that is important to her, every grandson would obey. So with great nervousness, after all, she received more fan mail in a week than most celebrities, I sheepishly approached Arlene one day on the show.

The moment I got closer, I lost my voice, my legs shook, and my heart actually began to beat faster. Not only was I now only a few feet from a *Bandstand* Regular known all over the country, but this young woman was truly beautiful...Elizabeth Taylor beautiful.

I know I asked her to dance, but I honestly don't remember saying the words. However, I vividly remember her answer: "I can't right now, ask my girlfriend Carole Gibson." I left crushed!

The irony was that I knew Carole and I had already danced with her. We both attended South Philadelphia High School, as did Frani Giordano, another well-known dancer and personality on the show. But my grandmother wanted to see me dance with Arlene and not Frani or Carole.

In my mind it would have been much easier to ask Frani, but then this story would have been years shorter.

Fast-forward several years and I stopped in the Holiday Inn at Fourth and Arch in Philadelphia to see a colleague, Fred Wahl, who was then VP of Marketing.

The first person I notice outside his office was Arlene Sullivan. I walked by and crisply said, "Hello Arlene."

A few minutes into my visit, Arlene buzzes my friend Fred to ask who I was. I guess the way I said hello made her think we had met. Of course, we did, but she could hardly be expected to remember that one moment in her life. God knows I never forgot that moment in my life.

After telling Fred the story, he asked Arlene to come in. I repeated the story for Arlene. She said she was surprised that she didn't dance with me because she always tried to do so when she was free.

Nonetheless, we laughed and continued to chat about *Bandstand* days when Arlene got up to leave and said, "Joe would you like to dance?" My response was sarcastic and a bit vulgar. I wanted to tease her a bit. It was basically, "screw you." She laughed and laughed.

Fast-forward a few more years and lo and behold, Arlene is working for another friend of mine. This time, Arlene is at Harrah's as a blackjack dealer. No, I'm not making this up.

After a few blackjack hands and some lighthearted conversation, Arlene would ask, "Joe, would you like to dance?" My reply was always the same sarcastic answer. Again, Arlene laughed. We had now established the "running gag." She would ask me to dance and I would tell her to "buzz-off."

Our next encounter is at the Cherry Hill Mall. She was with a friend and we stopped to talk. Of course, she related the original story to her and then all the additional meetings. This meeting was just a week after the opening of the movie *Peggy Sue Got Married*. I asked her how it felt to be mentioned in the movie using just her first name. Best of all, everyone knew who they were referring to on *American Bandstand*.

Just as we parted, Arlene asked, "Joe, would you like to dance?" After all these years, the question was the same, as was my flip answer.

When the year 2000 approached, Dick Clark had a party at his new restaurant and grill in King of Prussia, Pennsylvania. He wanted to take a picture as the millennium approached. I went thinking *this might be the night that Arlene and I get to dance*. Alas, Arlene never came. We took the picture. It was a great shot.

A few months later, I received a call from Carole Gibson about an *American Bandstand* get-together at the Pyramid Club in Philadelphia. I wanted to go because I hoped it would finally be the night I got to dance with Arlene.

When I arrived, I saw Arlene. The first thing she said was, "This is the night, isn't it?" I stammered, "Absolutely." She then added, "Let me ask you when there's a great song playing."

I heard a warm romantic ballad begin to play and knew this was the moment. She approached me and asked, "Joe, would you like to dance?" I finally answered, "Yes."

I'll never forget how she felt, how smoothly we danced, as if we had done so hundreds of times before. She paused for a moment and said, "Joe, you're an excellent dancer."

Grinning broadly, I replied, "Somewhere in Heaven, my Grandmother is looking down at us and smiling."

Joe Marrella (white jacket) at Dick Clark's American Grill in 2000.

The dance floor is busy—and so is Dick Clark, speaking with the control room on his telephone during a dance number.

The Regulars

Chapter 6

On *American Bandstand,* "Stars were born, fads were hatched, and a group of typical American kids danced their way into the hearts of all the show's viewers."

—Steve Brandt, *16 Magazine*

Bob Clayton

(1957 TO 1960)

Cool. Confident. Charismatic. Bob Clayton was the ideal all-American teenage boy. He was handsome, well dressed and had a movie star wave in his light blond hair. His appeal to *American Bandstand* viewers was instantaneous, especially female viewers.

His romance with Justine Carrelli reads like a fairy tale, too improbable to be true. But it was true. Bob grew up in Wilmington, Delaware, at least an hour's drive from *Bandstand*'s WFIL Studios in Philadelphia. After watching Justine dance without a steady partner on his black-and-white television, Bob decided that he was going to Philadelphia to make Justine his girlfriend.

Borrowing his family's black Chevrolet Impala, he skipped study hall, and drove like "a bat out of hell" to 46th and Market Streets. He was not going to the show to dance, or make new friends, or become a star; he was going with hopes of having Justine fall in love with him. But on that first day, Justine played hard-to-get, refusing to dance with him, at least for most of the day. *American Bandstand* was on for hours in Philadelphia; so by the end of the show, Justine and Bob were dancing together. The rest, as they say, is history.

The couple won one of the first dance contests on the show with almost a million postcard votes sent in. They won dancing that Philadelphia staple, and most popular dance in the city, the jitterbug. The grand prizes they won were his and her jukeboxes stocked with scores of 45 RPMs. Bob sold his jukebox for a hefty $1,000.

Every weekday, Bob and Justine danced on the show and mingled with the other Regulars; after the show they walked down to Pop Singer's to share a cherry Coke and talk with fans and other dancers. Bob often drove Arlene Sullivan and Pat Molittieri home on his way back to Delaware. On Saturdays and Sundays, Bob and Justine attended local dances in and around the city. Many of those dances, most held in Catholic Schools, held dance contests; Bob and Justine were popular, so they won many of those contests. Bob says the most they ever won was $100.

Bob had numerous fan clubs around the country, numbering about 500,000 total members. When he left the show, he was hoping those thousands of fans would help him become a recording star. He and Justine cut a record together; one side was "Drive-In Movie." The B-side was "Dream Girl." Dick Clark never played either song on *American Bandstand*. Bob's hope of a singing career faded, as did his popular romance with Justine. Bob had a roving eye,

Bob and Litzie with Barry Manilow.

Bob with his mother, Esther, and stepfather on his 86th birthday in 2004.

Bob and Litzie on their wedding day in 1985.

Bob and Litzie with Dick Clark.

Bob and Litzie at home.

One of Bob Clayton's fan club photos.

and Justine wanted no part of that.

In 1960, Bob had the opportunity to go to Hollywood for a screen test. The 5' 8" Clayton went west and stayed in Richard Crenna's mother's boarding house. Surrounded by 6-foot-plus wannabes, Bob realized that his chances for success were slim. He called home and asked his dad to send him money for a trip back to Delaware.

Back home, Bob went from show business to the shoe business. He sold shoes at Wanamaker's Department Store where scores of adoring fans gathered every day to get an autograph. He moved from Wanamaker's to his own stores, ultimately, co-owning four stores. Later, he went into the chemical business where he worked many 18-hour days. Today, he and his wife Litzie own a gift boutique, but he is a stay-at-home retired partner.

Bob says he is probably the opposite of who you think he is. "I'm quiet. I like simple things, and don't like big crowds." He doesn't use a computer; he doesn't even have an email address. In 1994, he had a heart attack. He was 54. He still suffers from hypertension. He had a drinking problem, but quit cold turkey in 1980.

Bob and his first wife had two daughters, one son, and one grandson.

During the Christmas holidays in 2013, Bob and Litzie were hosts to Justine, her soon-to-be husband Jim Miller, Justine's sister and brother-in-law, and some of the Clayton's neighbors. It was fun for the former couple to party together, especially with their significant others.

By the way, Litzie looks nothing like Justine.

"Every day is New Year's Eve."

—Justine Carrelli, "Eye to Eye," *CBS News*

Justine Carrelli

(1956 TO 1959)

There is only one Justine, known to her friends as Petey. She's the phenomenally popular and photogenic *American Bandstand* Regular whom millions of television viewers remember from her *Bandstand* days over 55 years ago.

Justine Carrelli lived in a Southwest Philadelphia row house with her father, a truck driver; her mother, a registered surgical nurse; a younger brother; and an older sister. While her mother and sister, Mary, liked the idea that Justine would be on the daily dance show, her father was more skeptical.

The junior high school student tried to get into the show at age 12, but was turned away by Bob the Cop. The next day, however, she got in by using her older sister's birth certificate and wearing makeup to make her look older.

Her first day on the show she saw Joanne MonteCarlo, Rosalie Beltrante, Peggy Thompson, and Barbara Marcen, who were all 15 and 16. "The aura in that studio was just over the top. I knew I wanted that," Justine told *Parade Magazine* in an interview in May 2012. Justine was awestruck and wanted to be "just like them."

Justine often wore beautiful hand-me-downs from several rich cousins. Her close friends who lived nearby included best friend, Pat Molittieri, and Little Ro.

She attended John Bartram High School and had perfect attendance and good grades. She focused on secretarial studies there, and a proud Dick Clark once showed her excellent report card on the air.

Clark seemed to favor Justine, choosing her for Spotlight Dances and record review interviews. Her favorite male dance partners, besides her steady boyfriend Bob Clayton, included Billy Cook, Frankie Lobis, Tony Porrini, Harvey Robbins, and Lou Solino.

The classic story about the Carrelli-Clayton romance started when Bob watched Justine dancing on *American Bandstand* from his home in Delaware; he wanted her to be his girlfriend. At the time Justine was dating Tex Connor. When that romance ended, Bob and Justine became one of the two most famous couples on *American Bandstand*; Arlene Sullivan and Kenny Rossi were the other. After the show, Bob would drive Pat Molittieri home and then go back to Justine's house. They did not socialize much with other Regulars outside of the studio because Bob wanted Justine all to himself.

Justine and Bob won one of the first *American Bandstand* dance competitions, the Jitterbug Contest. They won jukeboxes stocked with 45 RPM records; her unused jukebox sat in the basement until her parents sold it. While she was on *American Bandstand* she received tens

Justine performing with the Paul Dino Revue.

Justine signing autographs.

Justine at Pop Singer's Luncheonette.

Justine at Mural Day, 2007.

Bob and Justine with Dick Clark after winning the 1957 jitterbug contest.

At the beach with Justine's family.

Justine with good friend Billy Cook.

Justine after her wedding to Jim Miller in 2014.

Justine, the bride, getting ready to be married. Pat Molittieri is a bridesmaid.

of thousands of fan letters, dolls, jewelry, and clothing from admirers all over the country.

Her classic line was, "As I got more popular, I got blonder."

Justine loved show tunes and ballads and took singing lessons. She and Bob cut a record together called "Drive-In Movie," with "Dream Girl" on the B-side. But that broke the rules, so Tony Mammarella and Dick Clark ordered them to leave the show. Justine said the record was never promoted properly.

Their storybook romance ended when Bob's sister told Justine that he had "a roving eye" for other girls.

Eventually, Justine hired an agent and in 1962 was booked on the Vegas-Reno-Tahoe entertainment circuit. She later became the singer with the Paul Dino Review at the Fremont Hotel. Paul and Justine married in 1963 and had two sons.

Fast-forward to today. Justine is happily married to a *Bandstand* fan, Jim Miller, since 2014. When Dick Clark died, Jim Googled her and she agreed to meet him. They currently live in Mohave County in the hill country of Arizona with no nearby neighbors, 50 miles from the Nevada border. She still works in real estate, but rarely tells her younger clients about her famous younger years on *American Bandstand*. They just wouldn't understand the love and adoration that her television admirers had for Justine back in the day.

America's Sweethearts

BOB & JUSTINE

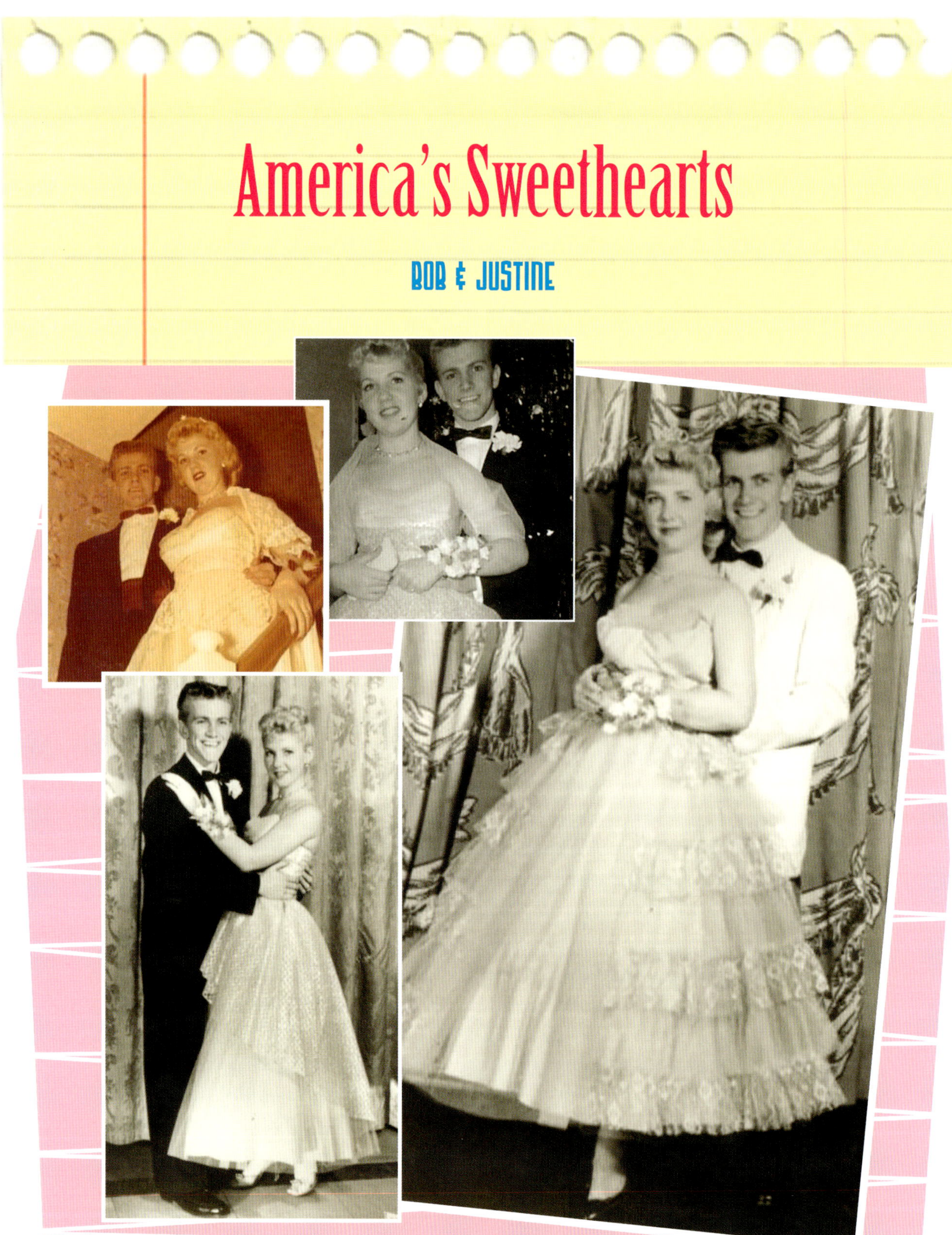

BOB & JUSTINE'S "DRIVE-IN MOVIE" RECORD.

JUSTINE AND BOB AT THE PHILADELPHIA STUDIO DEDICATION IN 1997.

Frani Giordano

1956 TO 1960

Francis Ann Marie Giordano is the bubbly blonde, hazel-eyed, photogenic, and extremely popular Regular who has successfully managed to stay out of the limelight for many years. We really don't know why but her fans would love to know, "Whatever became of Frani Giordano?"

Here's what we do know about her.

Frani lived with her father, Joseph, a buyer for his family's large fruit and produce market in South Philadelphia; her mother, Emma; two brothers, Felix and Joe; and two sisters, Anna Marie and Paula. She graduated from South Philadelphia High School.

According to her good friend, the late Pat Molittieri, she loved motor boating and skating. Her favorite singers were Fabian and Connie Francis. Her parents had a huge home in Sea Isle City, New Jersey, where many Regulars came to vacation during the summers.

Although she danced and flirted with many guys on *American Bandstand*, she did date Frank Levins and Denny Dziena. She has been married at least twice and has four children. Her first husband was Freddie Fantazzia, her teenage sweetheart.

Betty Romantini told us Frani has 13 grandchildren. We're sure that Frani must be a beautiful grandmother!

It is said that a picture is worth a thousand words, so here is the Frani we remember with love, from photos sent to us from many of her friends and fans.

FRANI MEETS HER #1, TEN-YEAR-OLD FAN

Shelley Savar was a determined ten-year-old fourth grader in Mt. Airy, PA. She adored *American Bandstand*, was infatuated with the Regulars, and joined them at home, dancing with her refrigerator door daily. *And*, she was determined to know the Regulars personally.

Frani near the phone booth at Pop Singer's Luncheonette.

The precocious Savar called 411 to get Pop Singer's phone number, which rang the telephone booth of his cramped drug store-luncheonette. But Pop Singer didn't answer that phone because he was usually busy feeding the Regulars either before or after the live show. Each day, a Regular would answer the pay phone and frequently would pass the phone around so Shelley would speak to different dancers. Shelley got the closest person to the telephone booth to answer her calls. It might be Frani or Pat or Carole Scaldeferri or Mary Beltrante or Peggy Leonard. She always said, "This is Shelley calling," and have chatty conversations with each of them. They would talk about what went on during the show that day.

Many of the Regulars even gave Shelley their home phone numbers. Frani's was FU 9- ----.

Yet nobody asked the ten-year-old her age. They thought she was a teenager just like themselves.

One weekend, Shelley, an only child, invited 15-year-old Frani to her parents' home In Mt. Airy for a home-cooked chicken dinner. She said "You can bring any of your *Bandstand* friends, too."

That Saturday, Frani and friends Pat Molittieri and Peggy Leonard stepped off the S bus to face a ten-year-old girl who shouted out, "I am Shelley!" None of her friends believed that a "national star" like Frani would come to their neighborhood, so Shelley invited eight young friends to meet and greet the Regulars and prove them wrong.

Although the Regulars were initially shocked to see such a young fan, they all had a great first meeting together. The teens did the latest dance steps in Shelley's living room to some of her 45 RPM records, while Shelley and her dad joined in. Her mother, like most mothers in the late 1950s and early 1960s, was in the kitchen cooking. Shelley recalled she was "in heaven." She couldn't wait to go to Pennypacker Elementary School the next school day to share the news with her friends.

After their meeting, Shelley continued to call her favorite Regulars at home.

Frani invited Shelley to visit her at home several times. Then, when Shelley was just 12 years old, Frani told Shelley to meet her at the *Bandstand* studio and she would get her in to the show. Of course, that was two years younger than the required age of 14 to attend.

When Shelley came into the studio with Frani she immediately was introduced to Carmen Jimenez and Louie Lucas, who were extremely friendly. The three danced The Strand together.

"I felt like I was in *The Twilight Zone*…I was in such a high…life couldn't get much better," Shelley recalled.

After that, Frani invited Shelley over to her home several times and also met her brothers, sisters, and Freddie Fantazzia, who would become Frani's first husband. Frani's mom, Emma, (who recently passed away), baked delicious Italian homemade pizza. Emma also showed Shelley the family photo albums.

Before Frani entered the Pony Contest with Mike Balara in 1961, Shelley taught her a few steps which Frani incorporated into her winning first-prize dance. One day, after Frani got her red convertible, she invited Shelley for a ride with her and Freddie.

However, over the years after Frani left the show and got married, they lost touch.

A few years later, Shelley's father, Dave Savar, launched a new business, The Jerry Blavat School of Broadcasting. You'll never guess who his secretary was. It was none other than Arlene Sullivan…

Shelley recently met Arlene again to film the *American Bandstand* studio for *Bandstand Diaries*. And now they're good friends so many years later!

Shelley visiting Frani at her home.

Arlene and Shelley, years later, at a reunion.

Carole Gibson

(1956 TO 1959)

Carole grew up with her older brother in an upper middle-class home in South Philadelphia. Her parents had one of the first television sets in the neighborhood and her mom opened her home to let the neighborhood kids come to watch kids' shows like *Howdy Doody*.

She remembers that Fabian, who lived three blocks away, went to school with her from first grade through all of high school. Her memory is so good that she remembers playing Spin the Bottle with Fabian and some classmates back in the sixth grade!

Her brother went to *American Bandstand* before she ever did and he showed her the ropes on how to get into the show. By the time she was 16, Carole was going with Frani Giordano to the show at least three times weekly. Before she became a Regular, Carole was on the shy side. Dancing and socializing on the show made her feel more popular and gave her more self-esteem.

During her last class period, Carole would set her hair and put a scarf over her curlers. Head scarfs for girls were very popular back then.

She remembers there was verbal abuse from some of her classmates who taunted her by saying, "There's the beauty queen from *American Bandstand*. Who do you think you are?" Sometimes Carole felt nervous and insecure, but she enjoyed her time on the show.

When Carole met Bobby Rydell at a Boy's Club dance, he was a year older. She had a school girl crush. They began to hang out together several days a week and she asked him to her junior prom. Bobby's father was their chauffeur. They had their first kiss at the Planetarium before he made his first recording "Kissing Time." And she remembers when they carved their initials into a table at George's soda pop store nearby Bobby's home. They went there frequently to get ice cream sundaes. Dick Clark often teased her about Bobby during commercial breaks in the show.

Carole went to cosmetology school and owned a beauty salon for some time. She became a dealer and supervisor at Atlantic City establishments—Playboy Casino, Caesars, Claridges, and the Showboat. Later Carole became a real estate agent.

Carole is now single, but has been married twice. She has five grandchildren. And she still sees Bobby Rydell at some of his concerts, where she chats with him backstage after the shows. Life is good for Carole Gibson.

Carole and Bobby Rydell at her junior prom.

Prom time for Carole and Frani Giordano.

Carole and Frani relaxing.

Carole with her family.

Carole with Dick Clark.

Carole with Bobby Rydell, all grown up.

Nino Bambino

(1956 TO 1958)

Nino today.

Nino with his *American Bandstand* girlfriend Rosalie Beltrante.

Nino and Diane Bambino.

Nino was the fifth of seven children born to a marble tile cutter father and mother in Philadelphia. He loved growing up and living in Philadelphia.

Nino was invited to *Bandstand* by Little Ro, who became his girlfriend for three months. He then broke up with her to date Big Ro (Rosalie Beltrante) for two years. He owned a black 1951 Ford Victoria and would frequently take Big Ro, Joanne MonteCarlo, Sid Payne, and Bob Durkin to different dances, including those at the Starlight Ballroom in Wildwood, New Jersey. He danced on the show at least four days weekly.

After high school, Nino enlisted in the Army and served with Elvis Presley in Fort Hood, Texas, before being stationed in Friedburg, Germany. Until 1991, Nino was a meat cutter for hotel restaurants for 40 years.

After Paul Thomas and Joanne MonteCarlo created the Alumni Association of American Bandstand Regulars, Nino became the producer of the events it created to help raise money for cancer groups and other charities.

Nino and his wife Diane celebrated their 50th wedding anniversary in 2016. They have three children and seven grandchildren. They live in Pennsylvania.

Ron Joseph (aka "RJ")

(1956 TO 1961)

Ron Joseph with the original Bandstand Billboard.

RJ with Dick Clark and Pop Singer.

RJ with Pop Singer on his TV show.

Ron Joseph today.

Ron was one of the early Regulars, starting out during the Bob Horn *Bandstand* days. Before he ever attended *American Bandstand*, he began his broadcasting career at age 10 on *Ghost Riders*, a children's show, and at age 14 he was a panel member on "Radio Rangers" on local radio.

Ron attended Upper Darby High School. Ron is filled with memories about Dick Clark and the show. He remembers going with Dick to personal appearances and, during the summer, to the Starlight Ballroom in Wildwood, New Jersey, where Clark had record hops. RJ is especially proud that Dick Clark was the only adult beside his parents and grandparents to attend his 16th birthday party with "65 screaming kids."

On one *American Bandstand* show, when Dick and Pop Singer gave him a birthday cake, Dick asked him "What do you want to be when you grow up?" RJ answered, "a DJ just like you."

RJ also remembers going to the Little Theater at 44th and Broadway in Manhattan for Dick Clark's Saturday night television program. One night, RJ had a bit part in a Beechnut chewing gum commercial right from his seat at the show. At 16, he appeared onstage with The Beatles and Dick Clark at the New Jersey Convention Center.

After high school Ron did a nightly top 40 music radio show. Ron also was on television with a show called *RJ & Company*, also known as "Disco USA." RJ has been in Philadelphia broadcasting for over half a century. His programs have aired locally and nationally on several different radio and television stations.

In 2007, Ron appeared in the movie *Fabulous*, the life story of Charlie Gracie, and in 2008 he appeared in *The Wages of Spin*, about the Philadelphia music scene from 1952 to 1963.

Ron is the only Regular to have had a show of his own similar to *American Bandstand*. He has Dick Clark to thank as his inspiration. And he also has Dick Clark's Top 10 Billboard from 1958, which Dick allowed him to use on his own shows.

Lou Solino

(1957 TO 1958)

Lou and Mary Ann Cuff.

Lou And Pat Molittieri.

Lou today.

Lou with Pat Molittieri and *Bandstand* fans.

Lou went to high school with Regular Chuck Zamal, with whom he still keeps in touch. He grew up with two sisters, but it was his mother who taught him to jitterbug. And he always wanted to be a dancer, or more accurately, a professional dancer. On *American Bandstand* he danced with and dated Mary Ann Cuff. He also dated Pat Molittieri briefly. Lou's *Bandstand* friends included Harvey Robbins, Joe Fusco, Frank Levins, Jimmy Peatross, Peggy Leonard, and Joanne MonteCarlo.

Lou is the only *American Bandstand* Regular who became a professional dancer. Lou left school in 11th grade to attend drama school and take ballet and modern dance classes. He moved to New York with little money and remembers eating oatmeal for three meals daily. At one point, he pleaded with his parents to send him money to live.

Lou studied at the Martha Graham School and studied ballet with the Joffrey School in Manhattan. His professional debut was at a Carnegie Hall performance where he was the only dancer on stage with 150 singers and one piano player. In 1968, he was invited to join the José Limón Dance Company for a two-week tour. It ended up being an eleven-year tour with the company through America, Europe, the Soviet Union, and the Middle East.

Lou met dancer/choreographer Paul Jenden in 1980 and moved to New Zealand to work with him. They were partners for 35 years until Paul passed away. Lou moved back to the U.S. in recent years and now lives in New Jersey.

Michael (Delfatti) DeLano

(1956 TO 1957)

Michael DeLano has the handsome good looks of a movie star, and that's exactly what he became after his days on *American Bandstand*. He was on the show when Bob Horn was the host and then when Dick Clark took over.

Michael Delfatti, as he was known when he was a 16-year-old from South Philadelphia (and then West Philadelphia), came on the show to meet girls and dance. He came in 2nd place with Charlette Russo in the Chalypso Contest in 1957.

In addition to dancing on the show, in 1954 and 1955 Michael also was part of two doo wop street corner groups in Philadelphia, The Fantasies and The Wonders. He actually appeared on *American Bandstand* in Philadelphia a few years later as Key Larsen with a Swan Records song called *"A Little Lovin' Goes a Long, Long Way."*

Michael entertaining.

Michael today.

Michael spent 45 years as an actor in Hollywood, and was featured in television's *General Hospital* and movies like *Ocean's 11* and *Commando*. He recalls playing sleazy bad guys for many of his roles. He also was a longstanding actor on the television show *Rhoda*.

After Michael and his wife moved to Las Vegas in 1992, he became a lounge singer, specializing in crooning the love songs that Frank Sinatra, Tony Bennett, and Neil Diamond sang during their careers. Michael still performs two or three times a month in Las Vegas.

The married father of two and grandfather of seven makes it a Sunday ritual to have pasta night for family and friends.

"My first impression was 'Wow! Look at how these teens dance.' I was a dancer in my hometown, but never danced like the Regulars. My vow was to learn the steps in front of the television, which I did!"

—Don Gillis, fan

Janet Hamill

(1957 TO 1960)

Janet had no idea she was remembered by *American Bandstand* fans until a few years ago when she Googled herself. She was, to say the least, shocked that Regulars like her still captured the public eye a half-century later.

Janet was the only child of a housewife and a mechanic from northeast Philadelphia. She appeared on the *Grady and Hurst* television show before she attended *American Bandstand*. Her friend Barbara Levick had suggested she attend.

Janet became a Regular the same day that Carole Scaldeferri did. She would do her homework on the subway after leaving Lincoln High School at 2:15 pm. Good grades were very important to her and her parents.

The popular blonde met and dated Tex Connor for three years. They won two dance contests, jitterbugging to "Tallahassee Lassie" and a slow dance one. Their prizes were boats and motorcycles.

Janet remembers having hundreds of fan clubs and being mobbed by fans who tried to overturn their Greyhound Bus going to a Dick Clark show in New York. She thinks all the fans wanted was a strand of her blonde hair.

Janet studied classical music for twelve years and wanted to become a classical pianist. Instead, she went to New York City and became one of the first Junior Petite Models. She did a lot of print work and commercials. She also enrolled in acting school after leaving the show.

Janet and Dewey on their wedding day, 1976.

Janet in a TV commercial.

In 1965, Janet beat thousands of women to appear as a mermaid in a national television commercial for Groom & Clean. It ran for three years. When the producers of that commercial discovered Janet was pregnant, they sewed a panel across the top of her mermaid costume because they thought she looked too sensuous. She also was featured on the covers of *True Detective*, *Modern Romance*, and *True Romance* magazines, making $150 an hour as a cover model. Her face adorned huge billboards across America and national magazines as a Benson and Hedges model with a cigarette in her mouth. And, Janet was a contestant in the Miss Rheingold (beer) contest in 1967.

Janet moved to California for work and dated Fabian ("a nice person, fun to be around"), Gene Pitney, Tony Orlando, and Jan Berry from Jan & Dean. She also was friends with Andy Williams, Paul Anka, and Ricky Nelson.

She performed at the Bay of Pigs for the U.S. Air Force, where she sang for the soldiers from the ship. It was there she met her first husband, Warner Blair, who saw her in the audience. "We dated for five years and got married," Janet said. The couple stayed married for three years.

Janet lives in Galveston, Texas, with her second husband, Dewey Meadows, a lawyer she met on a blind date. He swept her off her feet and married her four days later. Dewey waited to adopt Janet's daughter Kimberly Meadows until one year after they married because he wanted to make sure she wanted him as a Daddy. The couple celebrated their fortieth anniversary February 28, 2016. Janet recalls that everyone said the marriage wouldn't last.

Janet lives only ten blocks from her daughter. She had quadruple bypass surgery several years ago.

Janet continues to work, making porcelain Dresden dolls, including designing and making gowns for each one, and hand-built teapots. She also gives classes on making lace-draped dolls (it is a lost art), and handmade teapots and Christmas houses.

And, she's glad that so many fans still want to keep in touch with her!

Frank Levins

(1957 to 1960)

Frank Levins was one of eight children, the oldest boy in a tight-knit family. His mother, a homemaker, encouraged him to go to *American Bandstand* in the summer of 1957 after he had appeared on the local *Grady and Hurst* dance show for about six months.

Frank went on the show to dance and meet girls. He felt a "great sense of community, of being a part of something unique" when he became a Regular. He was not interested in becoming famous or popular, but he became one of the most popular and well-liked Regulars among fans.

Initially, he dated Frani Giordano for four months. When Frankie was 16, Pop Singer brought a birthday cake to the show and the crowd sang happy birthday to him. After the show, Frani and Frank walked down the street to Pop Singer's. She was holding the cake and suddenly asked, "Why am I carrying your cake?" And he replied, "Because I'm carrying all this mail/cards." At that point, she let the cake drop to the ground and said, "you carry your own cake." Naturally, they never spoke again.

Frank also had a serious romance with Pat Molittieri and they were engaged for two and a half years. However, they were not very compatible in their dance styles. She hopped and he barely moved, trying to be cool!

Frank's *Bandstand* friends included Larry Brumbach (whom he still sees frequently and has even traveled with), Harvey Robbins, Frank Brancaccio, Mary Ann Cuff, Peggy Leonard, and Arlene Sullivan (whom he dated "for a bit").

After going into military service in 1961—he served in the 82nd Airborne Division in Fort Bragg, NC—Frank studied at Spring Garden College and then graduated from Drexel University. He was a mechanical engineer for 40-plus years and retired in 2014, with the latter part of his career spent mostly in sales.

Frank was part of Yo! Philadelphia, a Labor Day weekend event at Penn's Landing in Philly, where many Philadelphia neighborhoods were represented. At this event, about 30 Regulars used to put on a show, which was led by Joanne MonteCarlo. This lasted for about five to six years in the mid-1990s.

A widower, Frank has been happily remarried to Elisabeth for 14 years. They met at a ballroom dance weekend. Elisabeth can dance but definitely not the *American Bandstand* jitterbug. They do ballroom and salsa.

Frank with Harvey Robbins.
Frank with Carole Gibson.
Frank on vacation.
Frank and his wife, Elisabeth.

Frank and Elisabeth live in Newtown, PA. He has one son, one adopted daughter, and five grandchildren.

Bob Bradley

(1957 to 1959)

The oldest of four children, Bob lived in Willow Grove, PA, 1½ hours away by el, subway, and bus from the Philadelphia *Bandstand* studio. His high school was closer to the studio, so his commute to the show was much shorter than his return home every night.

Although his father was dead set against him attending *American Bandstand*, Bob was curious. He remembers that the guys in his high school harassed him a bit, which he tried to ignore. His first dance was with Bobbi Young, and he also danced with Arlene Sullivan and sisters Joanne and Carmella MonteCarlo. He dated Carole Higbee for 2½ years.

Bob was lucky enough to be at the first national broadcast of *American Bandstand*. In the middle of the show, Dick Clark asked him and about 20 other Regulars and guests to line up. Dick handed each of them a congratulatory telegram and they were each asked to say which celebrity sent it. Bob was delighted to read the telegram from Elvis Presley because he adored the singer.

After school, Bob enlisted in the Army, went overseas to Germany, and worked undercover for many years. He lives in Florida, and is married with two children and two grandchildren.

"The Regulars made *American Bandstand* special. Everyone was friends. We were one big happy family outside of our traditional families."

—Chuck Zamal

Chuck Zamal

(1957 to 1958)

Chuck Zamal grew up in South Philadelphia, the son of a laboratory worker at Phillips Petroleum and a homemaker. He had one sister. At Bishop Neumann High School he was good friends with Lou Solino.

Before Chuck went on the show he danced to the music on the radio show *The 950 Club*, a radio version of *American Bandstand*.

On *American Bandstand*, his male friends were Lou Solino, Joe Fusco, Frankie Lobis, Bobby Durkin, and Sid Payne. Chuck was "head over heels" with Carmella MonteCarlo and dated her for two years. Often, a bunch of Regulars went over to Betty Romantini's house, where Betty's mother became a second mother to many of them.

Chuck was a nomad after graduating, living in Philadelphia, California, New York, St. Croix, and New Jersey. He became a hair dresser, then went into banking, worked on Wall Street, and finally became a graphic artist.

He opened a graphic arts business in 1971 with his friend Dom Alperti. Up until falling in love with Dom, Chuck believed he was straight. Chuck and Dom have been together for 46 years and married in October 2014.

Together, they live on three acres outside of Tucson, Arizona. Chuck loves to bake breads, cookies, and matzoh balls. "I love everyday" is his favorite motto.

Chuck with Carmella MonteCarlo.
Chuck with some members of his fan club.
Chuck and Dom.
The Zamal-Alperti residence.

Ivette and Carmen Jimenez

Carmen with Frankie Vacca.
Carmen with Kari Clark.
Carmen with Monte Montes.
The Jimenez sisters at a reunion.

The Jimenez sisters continue to be two of the most popular Regulars on *American Bandstand*. Ivette and Carmen were both born in Puerto Rico but moved to Philadelphia. The sisters had two other sisters and a brother. They attended Kensington High School.

Their most striking trademarks were the blonde-streaked bangs in their black hairdos. According to John Jackson in his book, *American Bandstand*, streaking hair became the rage among teenage girls. In later years, Ivette and Carmen opened up a beauty salon together.

Ivette danced on *American Bandstand* from 1958 to 1961. Her favorite dance partner was Ed Kelly. She loved to read and answer her many fan letters. Her favorite activity besides dancing was swimming. Jack Scott and Connie Francis were her favorite singers, Davey Frees remembers. She appeared on the Oprah show and at several Reunions in later years. She lives in Miami and has been involved in the real estate business for many years.

Carmen, who danced on *American Bandstand* from 1959 to 1961, sometimes put a red streak in her black hair instead of the usual blonde one. Her favorite dance partners, according to Davey Frees, were Ed Kelly and Mike Balara. She was also close to Frani Giordano. Freddy Cannon and Connie Stevens were her favorite singers; Robert Taylor and Rita Hayworth were her favorite actor and actress. Carmen has two sons and lives in Philadelphia.

We were unable to interview the Jimenez sisters for *Bandstand Diaries*.

"You knew you were a Regular when you got enough mail that they had to bring it to you in a box or a shopping bag."

—Betty Romantini

Betty Romantini

(1958 TO 1961)

Betty grew up in West Philadelphia with three brothers and an older sister. Her parents were middle-class, first-generation children of Italian immigrants. Like many families, Betty watched *American Bandstand* with her mother and her sister. When they watched Lenny Natale on the show, they all thought he looked very much like younger brother, Nick.

Betty went to West Catholic Girls High, which was directly around the corner from *American Bandstand*. So, at 14, she left her freshmen classes at 1:30 pm and would stand in line with some friends until she got into the show. She went specifically to see her favorite Regulars in 1956—including Arlene Sullivan, Justine Carrelli, Lenny Natale, and Joe Fusco—before the show went national. She still remembers how lovely Arlene Sullivan was as she always welcomed newcomers to the show.

Betty quickly became one of the "in" Regulars, a member of the Committee. Now she recalls that going to *American Bandstand* brought her out of her neighborhood to meet different kids than the Italian ones she was brought up with—rich and poor, Jewish and Protestant—from all over Philadelphia. Before that she said she lived in a sort of bubble, never getting to meet teens both similar and different from her.

Betty and Lenny Natale were the only Regulars to marry each other during the Philadelphia *Bandstand* years. Fans encouraged their romance and wrote her letters telling her how perfect they were as a couple.

Betty with Lenny and Debbie.

Four generations.

Family celebration.

Betty and her husband.

Recently, Betty was candid when speaking about their five-year marriage. "I was about 19 years of age when Lenny and I got married," Betty said. "Everyone would tell me how handsome he was," she said, "but after five years of 'perfect life together' I woke up and realized how unhappy and lost I was feeling." The couple had two children together.

Betty realized she was capable of more than keeping a clean home, being a good mother, and catering to her husband's needs. When she divorced Lenny, she was on a quest to find out who she truly was.

After Lenny and Betty separated, the single mother took a job as a waitress for several years. As her daughter, Debbie, and son, Darren, grew older, Betty began taking college courses. Then she became a child care worker for a group home for emotionally disturbed children. At that point she knew she wanted to be a social worker.

She also worked for 11 years as a Community Outreach Manager for a local hospital. Betty was honored for being an "angel of mercy," volunteering her time to assist elderly Jews in South Philadelphia.

Betty has stayed connected to many *Bandstand* friends through the years. Joe Fusco was the godfather to her daughter, Debbie, and Barbara Levick was her godmother.

Betty and her husband, Richard, have been married for 42 years and have one daughter, Erika. They have ten grandchildren ages one to twenty years old.

Larry Brumbach

(1958 TO 1959)

Larry grew up in North Philadelphia with an older sister and a younger brother. He lived one block away from Frank Levins, who has become his lifelong friend. Frank convinced Larry to go to *American Bandstand* after they danced on the local show, *Grady and Hurst*. They had also met Pat Molittieri at a local luncheonette, and she encouraged them to attend the national dance show.

On *American Bandstand* Larry was friends with most of the day's Regulars including Carole Scaldeferri, Barbara Levick, Peggy Leonard, Dottie Horner, Joanne MonteCarlo, and Justine Carrelli. His guy friends were Frank Levins, Joe Fusco, Frankie Lobis, and Lenny Natale. His social life revolved around the show and attending weekend parties and dances.

Larry's daughters Marissa and Jannine with Carter, Elizabeth, and Samuel.

Larry today.

He was in the slow dance contest with Barbara Magallanes the same year Joan Buck and Jimmy Peatross won.

Years later Larry attended Joe Fusco's dinner parties and said his friend was "a great organizer." He also attended the Reunion at Penn's Landing.

Larry was divorced after 40 years of marriage and has two daughters and three grandchildren. He often vacations with *Bandstand* buddy Frank Levins and Frank's wife, Elisabeth. Larry currently lives in South Philadelphia.

Terry Celie DeNoble

(1957 TO 1959)

Lou DeNoble

(1955 TO 1956)

A South Philadelphia resident, Terry loved watching *American Bandstand* because she wanted to be a professional dancer. As a youngster, she took tap and ballet lessons.

She watched the show daily and adored Rosalie Beltrante, admitting that she "wanted to be just like her." When she first arrived at the show, she and Carole Scaldeferri changed from their Catholic school uniforms in Sally Starr's dressing room. They became good friends, right up to Carole's untimely passing. She also became close friends with Joe Fusco and remembers his special catered holiday dinners for many of the Regulars.

Terry became a secretary in a real estate firm after high school.

Terry with Joe Fusco.

Terry with Dick Clark.

She's been married for 55 years to Lou DeNoble, a Bob Horn Regular. And she and Lou still go out dancing and jitterbugging every weekend. It's in their blood to continue the tradition.

Lou was a Regular on the Bob Horn *Bandstand*. He lived with his older brother, future singer Tommy DeNoble, and his parents in West Philadelphia. His father was a painting contractor as well as an artist and musician.

During his career he was a window dresser for major department stores in the Philadelphia area. He met his wife, Terrie Celie DeNoble, a Regular during Dick Clark's *American Bandstand*, on Wildwood Beach. They have been married for 55 years and still get together with the Regulars from the Bob Horn and Dick Clark dance shows.

> "I remember my mom saying if my grades fell I could not watch *American Bandstand* every afternoon. I ended up getting all As all through high school."
>
> —Luci Crittenden, fan

Joe Ahern

(1959 TO 1961)

Although Joe was a Regular *American Bandstand* dancer between 1959 and 1961, his professional life took him out of Philadelphia into the national spotlight of show business later on. (Drum roll please...Joe actually discovered Oprah in 1983!)

Joe grew up modestly as an only child but called his growing-up years "the greatest home life." On *American Bandstand* between ages 14 and 17, he remembers dancing with Susan Beltrante. His father drove a laundry truck and usually picked him up after the show. But sometimes his father was too busy to pick Joe up from the studio. Those days, Dick Clark, who had taken a personal liking to young Joe, would frequently drive him home in his bright red 1961 Lincoln Continental convertible, complete with suicide doors that opened from the inside. This definitely shocked the neighbors.

Fast-forward through a very busy career from the time he was a grill man cooking Philadelphia cheese steaks: Joe has managed television stations around the world, but when he ran Chicago's local ABC station, he helped launch *The Oprah Winfrey Show* out of *A.M. Chicago*. Currently, Joe is the Chief Executive Director of the "100 Club of Chicago," which raises money to help families of fallen first responders.

Joe is married and has three daughters. He lives in Chicago.

Donna Fusaro Druckman

(1959 TO 1963)

Donna lived in the northeast Philadelphia suburbs with her two younger sisters and parents. Even before she attended Bensalem High School, she took the 45-minute bus and el trip to *American Bandstand* alone at the age of 12. Her parents trusted her, and she would finish her homework on the train every weekday.

The first day she went, Jay Jacovini ran up to Donna on the line and said, "Are you Justine Carrelli's sister?" As she said, "no," he took her by the arm to the front of the line, saying, "Well, you are now." He introduced her to Carmen and Ivette Jimenez and Frani Giordano.

Donna would get to the show 30 minutes late every afternoon. But Donna walked past the lines, right up to Bob the Cop, who was sitting outside waiting for her, and he would open the door to the studio just for her. She ignored the lines of boys and girls still waiting in hopes of getting in the door.

Because Donna had gone to the show two years before she was 14, she ended up having her Sweet Sixteen cake on the show on her 14th birthday.

Back at high school, the kids tried to insult her, calling her "Miss Bandstand" to upset her. But Donna was a strong and confident young lady and names didn't faze her.

Donna with Michael Candolora.

Donna Fusaro getting ready to pedal.

Donna with her son Elias Druckman.

Donna met Michael Candolora and they became boyfriend and girlfriend. They recently spoke after 50 years apart and she admitted it was a great experience.

Dick Clark made Donna promise that if she ever cut off her trademark blonde ponytail that she would do it on *American Bandstand* with her father, a barber, doing the honors. She declined.

Donna is happily retired. In her working life she was a hairdresser, a cosmetologist, a court reporter, a mortgage broker, a funeral director-embalmer, an EMT paramedic (save the people rather than bury the people), an owner of four wallpaper stores in Florida, and an owner of a medical marketing company.

She has been married twice and has lived in Puerto Rico, Florida, and now Georgia. She has one married son with two doctorates—in psychiatry and chiropractic.

Single for many years, Donna is still looking for Mr. Right.

> "We were like miniature rock 'n' roll stars. We had fans, we had groupies."
> —Steve Colanero

Steve Colanero

(1959 TO 1962)

Steve with Mariann Tenaglia.

Steve celebrating his birthday with his adult children.

Steve today.

Steve lived in west Philadelphia and was the youngest of four children by thirteen years. He lived in a typical close-knit Italian family of the 1950s, which included his grandmother.

The first time he went to *American Bandstand* with five of his friends he was 13, but he was the only guy who wanted to return to the show. He remembers that Dick Clark grabbed him on one of his first days at the studio and announced on national television that Steve was the newest Regular. Suddenly, Steve was in a Spotlight dance with the popular Myrna Horowitz.

At his Catholic high school, the priests gave him a hard time for attending the show. But he did love dancing and his steady date was Mary Beltrante for two years.

Because there was no official dressing room or green room for celebrity guests to use, Steve would often accompany the male stars from the downstairs bathroom to the set. He especially loved Bobby Darin, who he idolized as a true gentleman.

Steve remembers one birthday when he needed two cabs to get him home with all the presents and cards he received. There were even some propositions from female fans—including a few married women who took a liking to him.

One time, during a cab strike, a bum with a long beard and raggedy clothes sat down next to him on the el. It turned out to be Dick Clark, dressed in disguise so people wouldn't recognize him.

Steve remembers Dick, a no-nonsense host, by the nickname he gave him, "The commander." Dick wasn't over-friendly with the Regulars and kept strict professional boundaries. "If you got in front of the camera too much, he'd call you back and tell you to circulate. In a nice way, he'd discipline us," Colanero recalled in a philly.com article after Dick Clark died.

Steve became a part-owner of the family business of heavy-duty highway contracting. They specialized in installing sewer pipes for bridges and roads as well as snow removal. He worked for 33 years, retiring at 51. Steve, a gourmet cook, also became a celebrity chef at The Sands Hotel in Atlantic City.

Steve has been married three times and has four children plus seven granddaughters and one grandson. His significant other is Mariann Tenaglia, who was president of one of his fan clubs over 50 years ago. They got together through Facebook several years ago when Mariann lived in Ohio. They live in Palm Beach Gardens, Florida, and also have an apartment in Italy that they visit annually.

> "This was Hollywood here. This was it."
> —Nicky "Blue" Fiorentino

Nicky "Blue" Fiorentino

(1959 TO 1961)

Nicky today.

Nicky learned to dance being the "doorknob" with which his three older sisters practiced the latest dance steps. They encouraged him to attend the show, where his frequent partner was Arlene DiPietro. They danced together in the Pony Contest. The tough guys in high school bullied him about attending *American Bandstand* and dancing on the show, but Nicky says Dick Clark became a role model for him. "He made me feel that if you want something in life, you have to be serious about it," he said in a philly.com interview. Nicky was a Teamster for 43 years.

Flossie Harvey Mancini

(1959 TO 1963)

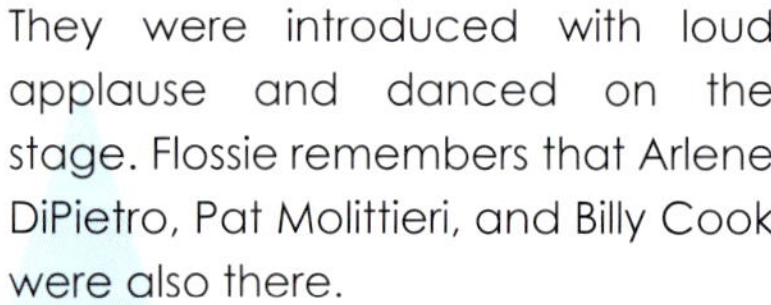

Flossie and Louie Lucas at the junior prom.

Frankie Vacca, Marlyn Brown, Flossie Harvey, and Donnie Coco at a prom.

Flossie and Louie with Diane Iaquinto, Tom Hogan, and Marlyn Brown at Flossie's Sweet 16 party.

16 Magazine photographed Flossie's Sweet 16 party at George Kralle's house.

Flossie and Bill Mancini.

The Mancini family.

Flossie was the youngest of six children born to a father who was an engineer and a stay-at-home mother. Because of the vast age difference between her and her siblings, she often felt like an only child.

Originally, Billy Cook, who was always visiting at her sister's house, suggested that Flossie visit *American Bandstand* and he got her a ticket to attend. Kathy Laferty was a classmate of hers and they arranged to go together. However, they both ended up wearing the same dress to that show.

She had a close group of friends including George Kralle, Mike Balara, Frankie Vacca, Vincent Friia, Carole Scaldeferri, Frani Giordano, Peggy Leonard, and Arlene Sullivan. Flossie also dated Louie Lucas for one year.

George Kralle threw her a Sweet 16 party in his backyard and *16 Magazine* photographed it for a three-page story.

Flossie remembers her days at the show with fondness. "The kids were like family," she said, and "we always had parties on the weekends in one of the Regulars' houses."

One weekend, she, Louie, Frani, and a date were invited to a dance show in Altoona, PA, and Frani's mother went along to chaperone. They were introduced with loud applause and danced on the stage. Flossie remembers that Arlene DiPietro, Pat Molittieri, and Billy Cook were also there.

The next Monday when she and Frani went up to the Regulars' entrance at the show, Bob the Cop stopped them. "You are barred from the show. You're not amateurs anymore," Bob said bluntly. Both girls looked at each other in astonishment.

From that time on, each week different Regulars were barred from the show. A new set of Regulars began to replace them slowly but surely.

Flossie married "the love of my life," Bill Mancini, 50 years ago at the age of 19. They owned a catering house, Mancini Caterers of Philadelphia, for many years until it burned down.

After *American Bandstand*, Flossie maintained a friendship with Joe Fusco, who had a Tuesday night dinner party every week that the Regulars were invited to attend.

Flossie was also a member of the Original American Bandstand Dancers that Joe Fusco orchestrated. They performed dance routines for many corporations and special events for a while. She also appeared in the movie, *The Twist*, which was produced in Canada.

Dennis "Denny" Dziena

(1959 TO 1961)

Denny grew up in Northeast Philadelphia with two brothers. His father was awarded two Purple Hearts when he worked as a radio transmitter and receiver for General Patton in the Battle of the Bulge in World War II. Later, his father joined RCA as a production supervisor in Camden, New Jersey, and his mother became a Republican politician after her sons grew up.

Some of the guys Denny went to Father Judge High School with had a running bet on who would meet and dance with Frani Giordano on *American Bandstand*. Since Denny was infatuated with Frani, he went to the show with his friend Billy Young hoping to meet her. His other good friend on the show was Joe Wissert.

However, Pat Molittieri introduced herself to him first. Even though it was only the end of the summer, Pat mentioned that the special Christmas show was coming up and the select Regulars who would be invited to appear on that show would be coming as couples. So Pat asked him to be her date and promptly told Bob the Cop that he was going to be a Regular.

Denny's mother had taught him how to dance, even the waltz, so when Alvin and the Chipmunk's Christmas song came on, nobody but Denny knew how to waltz. Seizing the opportunity, Denny grabbed Frani by the arm and suddenly a new romance bloomed.

Frani and Denny danced on the show steadily and he estimates that they went together for between 14 and 18 months. Both mothers got very close and Denny's mom confided to Emma, Frani's mother, that he was going to give her a ring to go steady. However, because both of them had big egos, they constantly fought. So even though were a steady couple, they didn't officially "go steady."

One afternoon when Denny had just left the studio and was already in the parking lot, he was accosted by three guys. One of them was Freddie Fantazzia, who told him that he dated Frani outside of the show. Freddie wanted to frighten Denny so he would leave Frani. A cameraman in the parking lot reported the fracas to Dick Clark the next day, and Dick called Denny into his tiny office. For the next two months Bob the Cop was in charge of taking Frani home and dropping Denny off at the el to get to his home.

Their romance ended after *16 Magazine* did a magazine shoot in New York with Frani and Arlene Sullivan. Denny's ego was bruised. He didn't know Frani was going to the photography session, and they never spoke again.

Denny led a charmed entrepreneurial life after *American Bandstand*, eventually owning several major companies as well as many Manhattan residential properties. He retired at 29 as a multi-millionaire. He was married for 35 years and is now divorced. He has a daughter, actress Alexis Dziena, an adult son, and a ten-year-old son from his current relationship. Denny lives in Kansas.

Anne Smith Lehn

(1961 TO 1963)

Anne grew up in Northeast Philadelphia with two brothers and two sisters. Her father was a musician; her mother worked in a factory. Her parents divorced when she was two years old. She went to West Catholic High School.

Anne had a curfew to be home by 6 p.m. for dinner. She began to dance on the show at 14 and left when it moved to California.

Anne's dancing partners were Steve Istak, Steve Lewis, and George Cherasaro. Eileen Wallace initially took her to *American Bandstand*. She was friends with Tony Origlio, Paula Kopicko, and Geri and Lorraine Ianetti while on the show. Anne worked in medical offices and hospitals after high school. She met her husband when he was singing in a club where her father was performing. Ten years later, the two got together and got married. They moved to South Carolina 24 years ago. The Lehns have two daughters and one grandchild.

Anne has been singing in a choir since 1972. And when she thinks about her feelings about being part of *American Bandstand*, her one-word answer is "joy."

Anne with her daughter.

Anne with her husband.

Marlyn Brown Kernan

(1960 TO 1963)

Marlyn with her dance partner, Charlie Hibib.

Marlyn with good friend Diane Iaquinto.

Diane with Frankie Vacca.

Prom time with Marlyn, Flossie Harvey, Frankie Vacca, and Frank's cousin Donny.

Diane Iaquinto, Judy Leibowitz, Charlie Hibib. and Marlyn Brown.

Marlyn and Jim Kernan with their grandchildren.

Marlyn lived in Northeast Philadelphia three city blocks from her close *Bandstand* friend Diane Iaquinto. She had one younger brother. Marlyn remembers watching the show when she was only six years old. She would dance next to the black-and-white television holding her staircase bannister, and her father would always remind her that she was loosening it from the wall!

Marlyn became one of the last group of Regulars on the show. She wasn't quite 14 when she made her first appearance on the show. Marlyn was a shy teenager, and felt the atmosphere of the show made her more talkative and outgoing.

Marlyn went to the show daily, especially after Regular Joyce Shafer kept on introducing her to more and more Regulars. In 1962, she came in second place with Frankie Vacca for the Mashed Potato Contest, winning a $1,000 wardrobe. She also went with Frankie to his senior prom.

As many of the Regulars were routinely invited to fans' homes, 14-year-old Marlyn was also invited to disc jockey Oakey Miller's home one weekend along with Diane, Alan Durban, and Vic Pracki. They took the five-hour train ride and danced on his weekend television show called *Altoona Bandstand.*

Marlyn graduated from high school at 17. She has worked at Sears Roebuck, for a psychiatrist as a receptionist, and as an administrative assistant for an insurance company. Her most recent career was working at her husband's credit union, where she retired in 2011.

Marlyn and her husband have two daughters and four active grandsons. They love traveling, visiting the New Jersey Shore, and, of course, visiting with their grandchildren.

Her friendship with Diane Iaquinto Celotto began in first grade when they were two of one hundred students in her classroom. The two still speak one to two times weekly.

Bob DiPietro

(1960 TO 1961)

Bob, older brother of Regular Arlene DiPietro, tried to get into *American Bandstand* several times in 1960 before Bob the Cop finally let him in. He got interested in going to the show so he could meet and eventually date JoAnn Franchi. But the first time he left the bleachers to go to the dance floor was when Arlene Sullivan beckoned him down, telling him that her mother thought he was attractive and that she should ask him to dance. He remembers that the guys from his high school who attended the show got a lot of flak and verbal abuse. Bob is retired from the pleasure boat and marine accessory industry. He and his wife live in Pennsylvania and have two children and two grandsons.

> "I think I'd stop going to *Bandstand* if I felt it interfered with my grades."
> —Diane Iaquinto

Diane Iaquinto Celotto

(1960 TO 1963)

A native of Northeast Philadelphia, Diane was an only child. Her dad worked on a factory assembly line putting parts in Philco televisions; her mother also worked on an assembly line in the food canning industry.

In the summer of 1960, two months shy of her 14th birthday, Diane and her best friend, Marlyn Brown, started going to *American Bandstand*. It took them almost one hour to get to the studio by bus and el.

She remembers some of her first dances were with Steve Colanero and Vic Pracki. Vic and she remained friends for many years; he even attended her wedding in 1968.

Even though she made friends with all the Regulars and was featured in teen magazines, Diane didn't feel like a celebrity. She loved dancing and meeting people from many schools and backgrounds.

She remembers Dick Clark as being very nice but firm with the Regulars. He was an authority figure.

Diane and Charles Hibib won third prize in the Mashed Potato Contest in 1962. She still has her prized piano.

Diane later joined Ed Kelly, Carmen Jimenez, Marlyn Brown, and Joyce Shafer and performed on a song-and-dance show called the *Radio Hits of 1958* on Monday June 30, 2008, at Town Hall on Broadway in Manhattan.

She worked in the accounting department of a cable and wire company for 22 years. Diane has been married for 48 years to Ronald. They have two daughters and two grandchildren. She and her husband live in a suburb of Philadelphia. And Diane is still best friends with Marlyn Brown after 65 years.

Diane celebrating her 15th birthday at the show.
Candid camera with Marlyn and Diane.
Diane with Charlie Hibib.
Diane with two of her grandchildren.
The Celotto family.

Anna Russo Bonanni

(1963)

Anna Russo was from South Philadelphia. She was one of the last Regulars who danced on Philadelphia's *American Bandstand*. She had idolized Arlene Sullivan when she was a Regular, but went on the show to meet Steve Lewis. They became close friends. After high school, she was a go-go dancer in Philadelphia. "Dancing was the love of my life," she recalled in the magazine *Primo*. A diabetic, she became disabled as a double amputee. She lives with her daughter and has an aide to assist her.

Michael Candolora

(1961 TO 1963)

Michael with Donna Fusaro.

Michael with his family.

Michael was an only child growing up in South Philadelphia. His parents both worked (rare in those days); his father drove a trolley and a bus, and his mother was a secretary.

Like many *American Bandstand* boys, Michael went there to meet girls. He danced with and dated Donna Fusaro for over three years. Yet his fame in teen and screen magazines didn't faze him at all.

After high school he joined a couple of bands and played the guitar three or four nights weekly.

Michael went to college at night while working days—first making helicopter parts, then as a butcher, and finally working himself up in the post office over 30 years, retiring as a supervisor in 2001.

The Candoloras have three daughters and two grandchildren. They live in South Jersey, about a half-hour from the *American Bandstand* studios.

Elsie Tillman McDonough

(1960 TO 1963)

Like many underage *American Bandstand* Regulars, Elsie, an only child growing up in Northeast Philadelphia, began to dance on the show when she was 12. Her grandfather always watched the show, and because Elsie was taller (5 feet, 8 inches), she got on the show easily. Her mother was especially grateful that she always knew where her daughter was because she could turn on the afternoon television and see her.

Elsie took the bus and el for over an hour every day to get to the show and remembers the final Philadelphia days when the Regulars would pack a suitcase with clothes as they taped five shows a week on Saturdays and Sundays. Her *Bandstand* friends included Michele Leibowitz, Bobby Baritz, Phil Maxwell, Aileen Silverman, and Joyce Shafer. However, she also had many Northeast Philadelphia friends who didn't dance on the show.

Elsie remembers that there were some high school girls who looked down on her or were jealous; she recalls that one girl attacked her in school and was suspended for it. She went to college for one year, wanting to be an art major and a dress designer. However, Elsie left and went into the insurance and real estate fields.

Elsie is married to her second husband, and has two children and one grandchild. From April to October, she and her husband sail on their 50-foot sail boat every weekend. They live in Pennsylvania.

Elsie today.

Elsie and family.

Arlene DiPietro Buccholz

(1959 TO 1961)

Arlene, known for her infectious smile and vivacious personality, lived in Drexel Hill. Her mother was a bank teller and her father was a welder. When her mother was home recuperating from an operation, she encouraged both her teenagers, Bob and Arlene, to attend the show so she could enjoy seeing them on television.

Arlene loved the idea of dancing on television in front of millions of viewers. Her very first time on air was a very overwhelming experience.

Nick Gaeta broke the ice for Arlene and asked her to dance. He also introduced her to other Regulars. But Arlene was more into studying than socializing, so she didn't get involved in partying much with the Regulars. She preferred the company of college-age guys and the neighborhood boys she often met through her brother. And she remained unaffected by the fame she received from fan letters and magazine stories that she was featured in.

Arlene remembers that one day a young man from Texas unexpectedly arrived at her house by taxi cab. Her mother took a liking to this stranger and invited him to stay with the family for a few days. The teenager offered to take over Arlene's chore of washing the floors, and Arlene agreed. He also went shopping with Arlene and bought her an outfit she wanted. Needless to say, this was quite different than if a stranger appeared on one's doorstep today!

Arlene graduated with a two-year associate degree from college and became a legal secretary. Afterwards she worked for the vice-president of the Philadelphia stock market.

Arlene as a young mother.

Arlene posing on her way to *American Bandstand*.

Arlene with Frank Brancaccio.

Holiday photo of Arlene, Sue, and their family

Arlene today.

She was married for 32 years, and has two adult daughters. Arlene remarried in 2015. She lives with her wife, Sue Petermann, in a Philadelphia suburb and together they raise and show dogs, including a top-winning Golden Retriever.

> "I was on *American Bandstand* on the very last day of taping in Philadelphia. It was very emotional for me and everybody else. We weren't happy with Dick because he was moving to Los Angeles."
>
> —Pat Kinzer Mancuso, fan

Rick Peterson

(1962 TO 1963)

Rick lived in Wilmington, Delaware, with one brother and one sister. It was a long trip by train and el, but Rick loved the idea of dancing on *American Bandstand*. He also looked like a twin brother of Richie Cartledge, and they became friends on the show.

On the show, Rick danced with Angel Mazza and Geri Ianetti frequently. Because he was on *American Bandstand*, when Rick went to local Wilmington dances he was mobbed by girls who wanted to dance with him, and guys who wanted to pick fights with him. Rick remembers having to slip out of bathroom windows at dances so he could escape the thugs who wanted to brawl with him.

Career-wise, Rick has been in the shoe and grocery businesses, a hair stylist, and a freight handler for UPS. He always had the acting bug, and since he retired in 2012 to a beach community on the North Carolina shore, Rick has been acting in commercials, television shows, and movies, mostly in background roles. He has one daughter and two sons, and looks forward to one day having grandchildren.

Thom Cardwell

(1960 TO 1963)

Although Thom was born in Philadelphia, he and his younger sister moved with their parents to the suburbs when he was five. He considers himself "half-Southern" because his father was from an Irish/Welsh family from North Carolina, while his mother was an Italian from Connecticut.

At Monsignor Bonner High School, a friend had two passes to *American Bandstand*. One afternoon he took Thom along. Thom fit in and thoroughly enjoyed himself. "I had a great time and met all sorts of people. I danced the whole show, and as we were leaving, they gave me passes to come back," he told *Philadelphia Gay News* in 2015.

American Bandstand also gave him a taste for the entertainment industry. He became a Regular and also began his career as a writer—as a ghost writer for *16 Magazine* writing gossip about the show, the Regulars, and their lives on and off the dance show.

Thom studied American and English Literature at Fordham University in New York. He began to organize film festivals as a college sophomore. Later, he studied film in graduate school and pursued a Ph.D. at Fordham.

Thom Cardwell with Barb Warchol.

Thom today.

During his active and prominent Philadelphia-based life, Thom has been a film producer, director, screenwriter, publisher, public relations guy, event planner, and columnist. He has been the developmental director at the Philadelphia Cinema Alliance, producer of qFLIXphiladelphia (the city's leading LGBTQ international indie film festival), and publisher/editor-at-large at *QUEERTimes Weekly*.

According to his Facebook profile, his motto to live by is, "Life is NOT a dress rehearsal." Certainly that is true for the dynamic Thom Cardwell, who has lived a very eclectic and intellectually prosperous life.

Tony Origlio

(1961 TO 1963)

Tony with Carol Channing.

Tony with his partner, Kip Vanderbilt.

Tony was a Regular on *American Bandstand* from 1961 to 1963. He moved to New York City in 1970 to pursue acting. Tony worked a bit off-Broadway and in television and film, notably performing in all the disco sequences of *Saturday Night Fever*.

Tony became a theatrical publicist and started his own theatrical public relations agency in Manhattan in 1979. He handled publicity for theaters, actors, singers, cabaret performers, and authors, including Milton Berle, Meryl Streep, Kyra Sedgwick, Hayley Mills, Mia Farrow, and Eartha Kitt, until 2006.

After he sold his firm, Tony and his partner of 34 years, Kip Vanderbilt, moved to the small medieval hilltop town of Orvieto in Umbria, Italy. He now divides his time between Orvieto and San Francisco with frequent stopovers in New York City to see friends and theater. Unfortunately, he has lost all his photographs of his younger days.

"*American Bandstand* was the reason that teenagers ran home from school every day, so they wouldn't miss a moment of the forever iconic show. Though long gone, long live *American Bandstand*!"

—Jackie West Grasso, fan

Ann Marie Maslan

(1962 TO 1963)

Ann Marie, an only child, lived in Chicago with her father, a crane operator, and her mother, a housewife. She convinced her parents to let her go on her first airplane ride to *American Bandstand* at age 15, and she stayed in a hotel with the late Marlene Mizanin.

She didn't miss a beat meeting the last Regulars of the Philadelphia era. She became fast friends with Richie Cartledge, Steve Lewis, Ailene Silverman, Myrna Horowitz, and Bobby Baritz. Many Regulars visited Ann Marie and Marlene at their hotel. Ann Marie has several hundred candid pictures of the 1960s Regulars in several photo albums.

After college, Ann Marie worked at the University of Chicago as a Cytopathology Lab Manager. She still lives in Chicago in a beautiful lakefront apartment with her cat Daisy.

Ann Marie with Richie Cartledge.

Al Demkowitz, Ann Marie, Marlene Mizanin, and Richie Cartledge.

Ann Marie and Daisy today.

Susan Selikson Markowitz

(1959 TO 1963)

Susan was one of the many Regulars who danced on *American Bandstand* at the age of 12, because nobody checked her ID. She took the bus and the Frankfort el every day with Michelle Leibowitz and Bobby Baritz from her home in Northeast Philadelphia. Marlyn Brown and Diane Iaquinto were often on the same train. "*American Bandstand* introduced me to a diverse cross-section of Philadelphia teens who loved dancing as much as I did," she recalled. Her favorite dance partners were Anthony Pannulla and Buddy Arensen. After high school, Susan became a hairdresser, then became a registered nurse specializing in geriatrics for 20 years. This proud mother of two lives in Houston, Texas.

Susan with her sister, Sammi, and her mother.

Susan today.

Whatever Became of...?

Barbara Levick
(1957 TO 1961)

Barbara Ann Levick was born in 1943. She had one brother, Ronnie, who is deceased. On *American Bandstand* she frequently danced with Walter Grzelak, Mike Balara, and Billy Cook. Barbara graduated Kensington High School. She won first place with Billy Cook in the 1960 Jitterbug Contest. Barbara, who has stayed out of the limelight, lives in California.

Joe Wissert
(1957 TO 1958)

Joseph Bryan Wissert appeared on *American Bandstand* when Frank Levins and Frank Brancaccio were on the show. He has become an internationally known American record producer, with credits by such artists as Earth, Wind & Fire, Helen Reddy, The Rightgeous Brothers, The J. Geils Band, Gordon Lightfoot, Boz Scaggs, and The Turtles.

Dottie Horner
(1956 TO 1958)

Dottie Horner has also stayed out of the limelight after her *American Bandstand* days. She did win the Chalypso Contest with Frank Spagnuola in 1957. She also danced with Jack Fisher on the show. Danny and the Juniors sang the song "Dottie" in her honor. Dottie did perform with many Regulars at Penn's Landing in 1988. She was working as a sales representative for a publishing firm at that time. Dottie and Frank also appeared on the front cover of *Dick Clark's American Bandstand* in 1997.

Doris Olsen

Doris Ann Olsen was born in 1945. The Drexel Hill native had a brother and a sister. She attended Upper Darby High School. Doris, a beautiful redhead with deep blue eyes, had attended previous reunions but was not reachable for an interview for this book. Doris has one daughter.

Geri Ianetti

Geri Ianetti Robinson was born in Northeast Philadelphia. She graduated in 1964 from Frankford High School. On *American Bandstand* she danced with Richie Cartledge.

Ronnie Verbit

Ronnie was born in Bayonne, New Jersey, in 1943. He graduated from Northeast High School. He currently lives in Southeast Florida and is a customer service specialist at a credit union. Since we had no contact information, he was not interviewed for *Bandstand Diaries*.

Frankie Vacca

Francis Michael Vacca was born in 1944, and lived in South Philadelphia with his three brothers and parents. He attended Bishop Neumann High in West Philadelphia, along with Louie Lucas and Frankie Ruggerio. According to *16 Magazine* his best friend was Peggy Leonard. Frankie's favorite food was ravioli and favorite color was green. His hobbies included dancing and collecting records. He lives in Philadelphia in a row home and still works as a hairdresser.

A happy Pop Singer holding court in his very crowded luncheonette filled with Regulars and fans during Bob Horn's *Bandstand*. Every day before and after the show, teenagers thronged both inside the corner luncheonette and outside on the sidewalk. It was a place to see and be seen.

Pop Singer and His Luncheonette

Chapter 7

Pop Singer

Simon "Pop" Singer was a loving and loved grandfather figure to the Regulars. *American Bandstand* fans frequently saw him on television when he delivered birthday cakes to popular Regulars on their special days. According to Regular Ron Joseph, "Pop actually came to the broadcast most afternoons."

Pop owned a combination drug store/ luncheonette a half-block away from the studio at the corner of Farragut and Market Streets in West Philadelphia. His cramped store and the sidewalk in front became the hang-out for the Regulars, the fans, and many of the celebrities who appeared on the show. After the broadcasts, the Regulars would stop by "Pop's" to grab a soda or a light bite before they headed home for family dinner.

Here are some photographs taken by the Regulars and their fans in front of his store between 1956 and 1963.

LUNCHEON
FOUNTAIN
SERVICE
SEP 60
Pop Singer
LUNCHEON
FOUNTAIN
Coca-Cola

LUNCHEON
FOUNTAIN
LUNCH AT OUR
Top Singer
LUNCHEON
FOUNTAIN
MOVIE
FILM
processing
Top Singer
LUNCHEON

Pat Molittieri.

Tributes to the Regulars

Chapter 8

Pat "Queen of the Hop" Molittieri

1943 TO 1979

Although Pat lived only to be 36, she lives on in the hearts of millions of fans who watched her inimitable dancing style, hopping and jitterbugging on *American Bandstand*.

Pat grew up in an eight-room house with her mother, Adele; father, Frank, who was a bus driver; and younger brother, also named Frank. She went to Bartram High School along with her close friend Justine Carrelli. Together they rode the trolley cars and buses to get to the *American Bandstand* studio, until Bob Clayton ended up driving them home after the show after he began dating Justine.

Her close friends included Billy Cook, Billy Ettinger, Frank Brancaccio, Peggy Leonard, and Frank Levins, to whom she was briefly engaged after leaving the show.

Pat's popularity soared after she collapsed in the hallway outside of the *American Bandstand* studio on August 9, 1957, and was rushed to the hospital with appendicitis. This happened the same week the show started broadcasting nationally. Dick Clark announced her illness on air the next day, suggesting that viewers write Pat get well wishes. She told *Teen* magazine that "hundreds of thousands of letters poured into the hospital, *Bandstand*, and my home."

Pat left the show in late June 1959 after Dick Clark called her into his cramped office, and behind closed doors, complained about her writing a *Teen* magazine column about the Regulars. As she received money for writing the column, Pat was asked to leave for becoming a "professional," which was against the show's policy.

After leaving the show, Pat moved to California where she enrolled at the Hollywood Professional School and continued writing her column for *Teen*. Pat recorded a song, "The USA," which Paul Anka wrote for her, while she also appeared as an extra in the popular motion picture *Where the Boys Are*.

Eventually Pat returned to her Philadelphia roots and met Victor Ranieri, a clothing salesman, whom she was married to until her death in July 1979. Pat's story of life after *American Bandstand* continues here with notes from our interviews with Pat's daughters, Dana Ranieri, who is a certified medical coder with two children, and Dellane Ranieri Develin, a teacher's aide for special needs children. She has three sons. The youngest, Patrick, is named in Pat's memory.

Pat Molittieri.

Pat with Lou Solino.

Pat with Bobby Burgess, whom she dated in Hollywood.

The girls were six and nine years old when their mother suddenly passed away during the July 4th weekend of a sudden heart attack. This is what they remember…

Pat's daughters describe their mom as a "very strong-minded mother—bubbly, vivacious, larger than life." She was a stay-at-home mom who was always involved in the girls' schooling. Pat was a class mother who baked cupcakes for special occasions and went on class trips with the girls and their classmates. The Ranieri home was often filled with friends dropping by for dinner as Pat cooked up pots of chili for the neighbors.

Pat always sang around the house, especially songs by Johnny Mathis and The Fifth Dimension. Naturally, Pat also danced around the house. Because she was double-jointed, Pat would often do splits for the girls while encouraging them to do the same. She encouraged her daughters to set goals and go for their dreams, frequently telling them, "you can do it!"

Pat had dated Bobby Burgess of *The Mickey Mouse Club* when she lived in Hollywood, and the girls remember their mom making them watch Bobby when he danced on *The Lawrence Welk Show*.

Dana and Dellane remember their mother would frequently make sketches—usually people's faces and scenes from *The Wizard of Oz*. She also did a number of Paint by Number artworks. They remember Pat saying she wanted "to become a kindergarten teacher eventually."

Although Pat had had a heart murmur, she was an active woman who swam, danced, and exercised.

Dellane feels "blessed and fortunate to be born to someone who is so loved to this day." Both daughters attended the *Bandstand* Reunion at Dick Clark's American Bandstand Grill in 1997. Dick Clark was so happy they came; they had dinner together as Dick shared stories about their mother—the one-and-only Pat Molittieri.

The family requests that donations in Pat Molittieri's honor be sent to the American Heart Association.

Pat with Fabian.

Pat in the recording studio.

Pat's single.

Pat and Victor with her parents.

Pat on her wedding day.

Pat and Victor.

Pat mothering Dana and Dellane.

Pat's Sweet 16 party.

Dellane and Dana with Victor, Pat's husband.

Remembering Pat

Pat was my closest friend on the show. She lived a few blocks from where I lived. I visited Pat's home frequently, as she visited mine. Our mothers were terrific together as they both were so proud of our teenage fame and all the attention that came with that fame.

After Bob Clayton became my steady, he'd pick me up in his 1957 Chevrolet. Many times Pat would come home with us. We enjoyed many years on *American Bandstand* until we were asked to leave the show—Bob and I for making a record; Pat for writing magazine articles.

Pat went off to California to further her career and I went to Las Vegas to sing and dance. We were not in very close contact while working on our careers. The bond of friendship was there, nonetheless, and Pat was in my wedding party in 1963.

My heart was broken when I heard Pat had passed away at such an early age. I wish we would have been in closer contact after we both got married.

If you have a close friend, please don't ever let time and distance separate you.

Justine Carrelli-Miller

Pat as a bridesmaid at Justine's first wedding.

As long as we love,
they too will love;
for they are now
a part of us as we
remember them.

Carole Scaldeferri Spada

1943 TO 2013

Carole appeared on *American Bandstand* from 1957 to 1961. We interviewed her in early December 2013, one week prior to her sad, sudden death because of congestive heart failure. Time and again, each of the Regulars we spoke with always had the kindest comments about her. Carole truly was loved by her peers, as well as millions of fans throughout the years.

Carole Ann Elizabeth Scaldeferri grew up with an older brother, Bill, and her parents, John and Sarah, in a large house in Philadelphia. She relished her three bedroom closets as they were always filled with the lovely outfits she wore both on and off screen. Carole was definitely a fashion plate known for her stylish clothing as well as the headband look she frequently wore in her beautiful long black tresses.

Carole told us she learned to dance from the African-American girls she knew in West Catholic Girls High School. At 13, she often left school a little early so she could get into the *American Bandstand* studio. Her intention was to meet her idol Sal Mineo. When she soared in popularity, receiving 500–600 fan letters a week, she became a Regular. She remembers that a group of secretaries acted as censors, opening the Regulars' fan mail before they received it.

Because Carole always changed into the latest fashions instead of wearing her parochial school uniform, she was assigned to change in a dressing room formerly used by Sally Starr.

Her profile in one of the teen magazines said her favorite dance partners were Mike Balara and Don Cione. Another favorite dancing partner was Harvey Robbins. Her hobbies including reading and writing poetry. She loved to swim. And Carole absolutely adored her mother's homemade lasagna. Her favorite singers were Johnny October and Annette. She loved Frank Sinatra and Shirley MacLaine for their acting. One magazine reported that Carole "was seriously considering becoming a nun, but has decided she would be happiest being a model or teacher." She spent one year at college to become a children's counselor, but decided instead to become a real estate agent.

Carole and her second husband, Richard Spada, were married in 1977 after a whirlwind courtship. They owned a beauty salon.

Carole is survived by her husband; daughter, Andrea Pergolese; four grandchildren; and a great granddaughter. She is also survived by millions of fans who remember her as one of the most gracious and popular Regulars to appear on *American Bandstand* in its Philadelphia heyday.

Carole in front of Pop Singer's Luncheonette.

Carole with Susan Beltrante.

Carole with Don Cione.

Carole with Larry Giuliani on the dance floor.

Carole and Arlene.

Get together with Irene Mariano, Denny Dimas, Carole Scaldeferri, Carol Marone, Vincent Miccicci, Don Clone, and Bonnie Harden.

A Love Letter to Carole

When I was fourteen, I, like many other teenagers, watched *American Bandstand.* I saw the most beautiful girl dance by the screen, and my heart fluttered. As the camera stayed focused on her, I knew at that moment I wanted to meet her, and I prayed to God to make a way that I would.

Like all the other fellows in Middletown High School in Connecticut, I had a picture of Carole Ann Scaldeferri in my locker. My grandmother knew of my infatuation and suggested I draw a picture of Carole and send it to the *Bandstand* Studio. She said that she might not be alive to see it, but that one day I would meet Carole.

I drew a picture of Carole with colored pens and sent it to the studio. Maybe six weeks or so went by and then, one afternoon, my Grandmother called me to the television set. Dick Clark had the picture in his hand on the television show and was showing it to Carole. She smiled. I was so excited tears poured out of my eyes and my heart was full of joy.

I thought that maybe I might hear from her. But I didn't. My grandmother looked at me again and predicted that one day she may become your wife.

In mid-1977, I was working in a well-known Los Angeles bookstore, World Book and News. My boss who I was very close to showed me a magazine article about celebrities who were no longer in the limelight. I saw Carole's beautiful photo, and my heart fluttered again. My boss turned to me, touching his stomach, and said, "You're supposed to meet this girl. Write her a letter."

So I decided to write a short note to Carole in care of Dick Clark Productions in Los Angeles and delivered it there personally.

Carole is a very private person and, even during her days on *American Bandstand*, did not personally answer her fan mail. However, in about a month, I received a letter from Carole and it was filled with beautiful pictures of tulips and violets. We corresponded for a while and then Carole suggested that she had a good friend out in Los Angeles whom she would like me to meet. We did meet and he got to know me better; he recommended to Carole that she should definitely meet me.

One day, I decided to send her my phone number. That night I received a phone call, and the voice on the other end of the phone said, "This is someone from your past." It was Carole, at last.

Shortly afterward, in July, I was going to visit my parents in Connecticut and asked Carole if it would be all right if I stopped off at the Philadelphia airport at 10 a.m. for breakfast with her and then I would take another airplane to my parents' home in Connecticut at 2 p.m.

Well, we met at the airport for the first time. "I've waited so long to meet you," I said. She smiled.

I touched her hand and felt like I had known her all my life. And I knew she was my wife. I later learned Carole felt the same way.

I decided to stay one more day with Carole, to see the Liberty Bell, to see the Betsy Ross House, and to be with Carole. Four months later, we married.

I once asked Carole why she never responded to the picture I had drawn of her that Dick Clark showed on *American Bandstand.* Carole looked at me, smiled, and said, "It wasn't the time!"

And I was blessed for almost thirty-seven years of pure ecstasy and unspeakable joy. Her memory is alive in my heart and soul forever!

Love,
Richard

Carole and Richard Spada two weeks after their honeymoon, while visiting his parents in Connecticut.

A more recent photo of Carole and Richard.

Myrna Horowitz

1942 TO 2009

Myrna was well-known and extremely popular among both the Regulars and fans. Myrna stood out from the rest of the dancers because she wore a leg brace and limped from her bout with polio at age seven. However, she never let her impairment interfere with her many activities on and off the dance floor during her *American Bandstand* years from 1957 to 1959.

Myrna went to *American Bandstand* only because Harvey Robbins, her good friend, told her Tab Hunter was going to appear one day. At first she went occasionally, until the summer of 1957 when she danced every day.

On her 16th birthday, February 25, 1958, Myrna was invited to become a member of the "Committee." She told *Teen* readers, "It was an exciting experience; one where you got to know Dick really well." Later that year, Dick Clark disbanded the group, replacing it with the Bandstand Chapter of the Dick Clark Fan Club, with Carole Higbee as president.

Myrna adored Freddy Cannon and ran one of his fan clubs. Her all-time favorite song was The Teddy Bears' "To Know Him is to Love Him." She graduated from West Philadelphia High School. Afterward, Myrna enrolled at Temple University's Community College to become a private secretary. In Philadelphia she worked at Swan Records and for the local government. Myrna was also invited to write a column for *Teen Screen Magazine*. It evolved into a popular four-page section of the magazine. Along with Justine Carrelli and Joe Fusco, Myrna appeared on *3rd Degree*, a 1989 quiz show.

Myrna later moved out to California. She was close friends with the late Regular Marlene Mizanin, and they stayed in touch with each other for almost 50 years.

Pat Molittieri wrote about Myrna in *Teen Magazine*, saying, "I've never met a person with so much faith in herself and the world around her." Pat called Myrna "one of my fondest *Bandstand* buddies."

Myrna passed away in 2009. She is gone, but certainly not forgotten.

Myrna Horowitz.

Myrna and Harvey Robbins.

Myrna and Jerry Blavat.

Myrna at her office working.

Myrna and Dion.

Myrna with Eddie Kelly.

Myrna with Regular Marlene Mizanin and Freddy Cannon and his wife.

Myrna with Dick Clark and Charlie O'Donnell.

Myrna and Bobby Baritz.

Billy Cook

1942 TO 1992

William John Cook, Jr. lived with his parents and sister in Lester, Pennsylvania. He graduated from Bishop Neumann High School in 1960. Known for his ever-present grin, he was one of the top male dancers on the show. His frequent partners were Barbara Levick and Pat Molittieri. He and Pat were close friends for many years.

Billy appeared on a record cover with Justine Carrelli (*Rock-A-Ballads*). He tried his fame as a singer, cutting a record on the Lawn label called "Mystery Girl." The flip side was "This Little World." Later, Billy worked with Dick Clark on some of his celebrity road shows. He also handled bookings and operations for the Philadelphia Civic Center.

Tommy DeNoble

1939 TO 2004

Tommy was a South Philadelphia native who was one of the original *Bandstand* Regulars from 1953 through 1956 when Bob Horn and Lee Stewart hosted the show.

After becoming a popular dancer on the local show, Tommy created a singing group called The Stardusters. When Bob Horn discovered Tommy had a voice like Eddie Fisher, he introduced Tommy to Jerry Ross, a record producer, who launched his singing career in 1957 with "Count Every Star." Dick Clark invited him to sing it on *The Dick Clark Show*.

Tommy also performed on *The Children's Hour* and played the role of Sgt. Sacto on a Philadelphia-based children's show. He appeared in several movies, including *The Monkey's Uncle* and *Ship of Fools*.

Eventually, Tommy became a television engineer for WTAF television, where he worked for over three decades.

Tommy died in 2004, and was survived by his wife, Loretta, and three sons. His brother, Regular Lou DeNoble, also survives him. Tommy was inducted into the Philadelphia Broadcast Pioneers' Hall of Fame posthumously in 2011.

Paula Kopicko

1947 TO 2007

Paula was known affectionately as "Mighty Mouse" because of her petit stature at 4'10" and her frenetic dance style. She lived in South Philadelphia and loved dancing with her favorite dance partner, Richie Cartledge. Her close girlfriends included Marlyn Brown and Joanne Hall. She had two children and three grandchildren.

Norman Kerr

D. 12/6/1990

Norman was known to *American Bandstand* fans as Joyce Shafer's close friend and steady dance partner. He grew up in New Jersey. He started going to the show in June 1959 because of his love for dancing. The show also offered him something special to do in the afternoons after school. Norman's secret desire was to go to California and attend acting school.

Jay Jacovini

1944 TO 2010

Joseph Robert Jacovini, known since grade school as Jay, attended Southern High in Philadelphia while appearing on *American Bandstand*. He lived in South Philadelphia with his mother, two brothers, and sister.

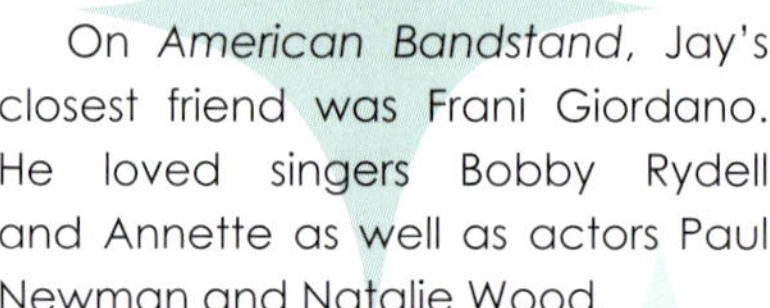

On *American Bandstand*, Jay's closest friend was Frani Giordano. He loved singers Bobby Rydell and Annette as well as actors Paul Newman and Natalie Wood.

At the time of his death at 65, Jay was working at Tampa's Seminole Hard Rock Casino. He is survived by a son, Jamison, and his life partner, Jean.

Richie Cartledge

1947 TO 1991

Richie was one of the most popular 1960s Regulars. He first went to *American Bandstand* in the summer of 1962, where he met Paula Kopicko the first day he attended. He and Paula won first place in the Mashed Potato Contest. Geri Ianetti was another favorite dance partner.

Richie attended John Bartram High School and wanted to be a commercial artist when he grew up. He was very good friends with the late Marlene Mizanin and Ann Marie Maslan, whom he visited at home in Chicago during vacations.

Larry Giuliani

1940 TO 2002

Larry was on *American Bandstand* from 1957 to 1960. He appeared with several Regulars when they were featured on *The Oprah Winfrey Show*. He owned a hair styling salon in Lancaster, Pennsylvania, for 29 years before he died unexpectedly at 62.

Bruce Richard

After a stint as a model, Bruce became Peggy Lee's hairdresser. He died in the mid-1980s.

Mary Ann Cuff LeGrand

1942 TO 2010

Mary Ann rushed to the *Bandstand* studio every afternoon from West Catholic High School for Girls. While the popular Regular appeared on *American Bandstand* from 1956 to 1961 she dated Lou Solino. She first worked as a secretary and then as a waitress for 33 years. In 1995, she reunited with other *Bandstand* Regulars at the Yo Philadelphia Festival on Penn's Landing. A Minnesota resident, Mary Ann had two children, four stepchildren, fourteen grandchildren, and eight great-grandchildren. She died at 68 in 2010.

Don Cione

Dominic John Cione's most frequent dance partner was Carole Scaldeferri, whom he danced with in the 1960 Jitterbug Contest. According to his high school yearbook, his secret ambition was to be the owner of a Lincoln Continental. He also wanted to be a model of men's clothing, and to be remembered for originating new dance steps.

Joe Fusco

Joe appeared on *American Bandstand* between 1958 and 1960. The popular dancer, a hair dresser, stayed friendly with many Regulars long after the show was over. He was godfather to Betty Romantini's daughter. Joe was known for the extravagant Tuesday night dinners he created for many Regulars. He also helped organize the *American Bandstand* Original Dancers.

Rebecca "Becky" E. LaSpada

1942 TO 2016

Becky was on both *Bandstand* and *American Bandstand*. Sometimes she left the studio with Dick Clark and they took the el together. She was neighbors with Frank Brancaccio as well as Frankie Avalon, Bobby Rydell, Fabian, and Chubby Checker in South Philadelphia. During live commercials, she and Mary Ann Cuff would frequently try to distract Dick Clark with funny pranks.

After high school, Becky joined the Marines. She became a waitress for many years before becoming a counselor at a center for abused women and children. She was still working as a school bus aide for disabled children at the time of her death in 2016 from lung cancer. Becky left behind many friends who loved her spunky sense of humor and good-natured personality.

Marlene Mizanin

1945 TO 2016

Marlene was born and raised in Chicago. During her high school years, she travelled to Philadelphia frequently to dance on *American Bandstand*. She became lifelong friends with Myrna Horowitz and Ann Marie Maslan.

After moving to California in 1979, Marlene began working for the City of Palmdale.

After her retirement as Director of Human Resources in 2004, Marlene returned to her hometown of Chicago. She left an extensive collection of photos she took of the Regulars to her friend Ann Marie Maslan.

Carmella Astrella

1947 TO 2016

Carmella was on *American Bandstand* from 1961 to 1963 (from age 13 to 15). She remembered growing up in South Philadelphia as the best childhood, until her father was killed in a car accident when she was just 13.

She wanted to quit school and become a dancer, but wisely thought better of that. After high school, Carmella worked in a bank and did office work. She met her first husband while a senior in high school. She married a second time and was divorced from her second husband.

Carmella had three daughters and five grandchildren.

Frankie Lobis

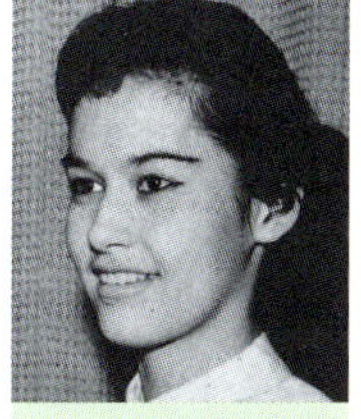
Barb Magallanes
(d. 0/5/2012)

Bill "Speedo" Mulvihill
(d. 3/13/2003)

Billy Young

Mike Balara
(d. 11/11/2001)

Bonnie Harden

Monte Montes

Charlie "Rubber Legs" Hibib

Jimmy Peatross
(d. 1/31/2011)

Joan Buck
(d. 6/16/2001)

Bob Kelly
(d. 12/11/1987)

Joe Sullivan

Joe Venuti

Harvey Robbins

Lorraine Ianetti (Mankowski)
(d. 3/1/1973)

Bobby Baritz
(d. 11/16/1991)

Carmella MonteCarlo

Joanne MonteCarlo Armstrong
(d. 1/30/2011)

Nick Gaeta
(d. 1977)

Paul Thomas

Phil Maxwell
(d. 1/18/2006)

Sandi Short

Steve Lewis
(d. 12/2008)

Walter Grzelak
(d. 6/3/2003)

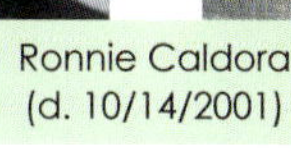
Ronnie Caldora
(d. 10/14/2001)

We Also Remember

Lynn Boehmer

Lillian Bonsera

Joey Cain

Pat Carpino (unconfirmed; details unknown)

Mary Ann Cocelle (d. 2008)

David "Big Dave" Feldbaum (d. 6/25/2012)

Bill Ettinger (d. 9/5/2016)

Vincent Friia

Bruce Kaplan (d. 12/28/2009)

George Kralle

Peggy Leonard (d. 1/13/2004)

Ronnie Levick (d. 6/14/2009)

Alan Levin (d. 12/25/2005)

Louie Lucas

Allyn Markert (d. 11/20/2015)

Kathy McClogan

Norm Miller

Vic Pracki (d. 8/1/1995)

Pop Singer (d. 12/27/1979)

Gary Stapleford (d. 7/15/2004)

The Little Theater on 44th Street in New York City. Dick's Saturday night show came from here and it was outside the theater that hundreds of *American Bandstand* fans surrounded the Regulars a little too enthusiastically. Police had to escort them into the show.

FAN-tastic Bandstand

Chapter 9

American Bandstand Fan Clubs

BY STEPHANIE HAMMONDS

Like so many of my fellow baby boomers, I grew up watching *The Mickey Mouse Club* and danced along as Annette Funicello and Lonnie Burr tapped their ways into our hearts. It was the fabulous 1950s—the years after World War II when radios brought swing and big band music to the masses.

Teens lined up each afternoon to attend *American Bandstand*. This line is much smaller than usual.

In August of 1957, *Bandstand*, a local music show in Philadelphia, became the nationally syndicated show *American Bandstand*. It showcased popular entertainers, including the handsome and charismatic host, Dick Clark. Dozens of Philadelphia teens made their ways to the corner of 46th and Market Streets in West Philadelphia to dance to the latest hits.

American Bandstand attracted a vast audience made up of thousands of teens and their families. Everyone who was at home after school rolled back the rug, warmed up the black-and-white TV, and tuned in to the most popular daytime show. Dinner plans and homework assignments would have to wait—it was time for *American Bandstand*.

As the records spun, new dances came out almost weekly. Watching the Regulars' fast footwork kept record hops and Friday night dance parties alive all over. While they did the jitterbug, the cha-cha, and the twist, we danced right along with them. We watched intently to learn every step; we noticed every couple, every move, and all of the hair and fashion trends.

The Regulars became as popular as movie stars, adorning magazine covers and becoming the subjects of endless interviews and articles. They were ordinary teens who had suddenly transformed into celebrities. In every town, soda shops sprang up with burgers, ice cream, cokes, and jukeboxes. Philadelphia was no exception; "Pop" Singer's shop near the studio offered the Regulars a place to hang out before and after the show. Singer's shop also gave journalists and fans a place to meet and photograph the most famous teens in the country.

The process of viewers getting to know the Regulars had begun with Dick Clark's segments like record review and the spotlight dance, when he would ask a Regular for their name, age, and school. Once the viewers learned a Regular's name, they could look for a fan club to join.

Although we lacked the Internet and other modern technology, our magazines, letters, and fan clubs sped information to untold thousands of fans. Our communication took the form of paper, pens, stamps, and envelopes. It was not only an exciting process to communicate with other fans all across the US and Canada who shared the same interests, but it was a truly enjoyable pastime. The postman was my hero; he arrived each day with piles of up to fifty letters for me. I wrote not only to my pen pals, but also to the Regulars, who wrote back.

I still remember when I got my very first letter from a Regular: Frani Giordano. It was written in pencil on plain paper and folded into thirds. I must have read it one hundred times. Other letters came from Barbara Levick, Janet Hamill, and Carole Scaldeferri. Those letters were precious to me, like silver or gold. The Regulars were peers and role models—girls who attended high school, went bowling, got their hair cut and set, and made time to be on *American Bandstand*.

I was one of the many teens who ran fan clubs for the Regulars, my first being for Frani Giordano. To run a fan club meant gathering information and sending out a fan club package to an interested member. The membership costs were somewhere between a quarter and a dollar each. The packages included stock items, like a photo signed by that Regular (either personally or stamped) and a fact sheet that provided details about his or her personal life, school, and likes and dislikes.

Teen magazines such as *'Teen*, *Dig*, *Teen World*, and *16 Magazine* would publish lists of current fan clubs. The Regulars' fan clubs were featured alongside those for stars like Frankie Avalon, Connie Stevens, and Natalie Wood. Arlene and Bob DiPietro, Thom Cardwell, Terri Cellie, Betty Romantini, Arlene Sullivan, Kenny Rossi, Doris Olsen, Justine Carrelli, Bob Clayton, the Leibowitz sisters (Judy and Michele), Joyce Shafer, Norman Kerr, Steve Colanero, and the Beltrante sisters (Mary and Rosalie) were just a few of the many who had their information in my albums.

As fan clubs were printed in various teen magazines, referrals went back and forth from teens who had joined them or who had connections through pen pals. After my name and address were printed in the pen pal column of *'Teen* magazine in April 1959, my number of pen pals grew to hundreds. Sometimes we would exchange memberships in each other's fan clubs.

We paid the fees for our own photo processing and most of the information sheets, which would only cost a few cents to reproduce. The photos were usually provided by the Regulars themselves or another fan club president who would share their stock. It was typical to buy twenty-five reprints for one dollar, which included postage.

As fan club presidents, we often got involved with Regulars' birthdays. Dick Clark would sometimes have a cake brought to the show, but when we learned the birthday of our favorite Regulars, we showed our appreciation by sending gifts. There were so many Regulars that at least one of their birthdays fell on each week. One year, I sent Frani Giordano a hoodie cardigan sweater in lavender (one of her favorite colors) as a present, and she wore it on the show on her birthday. I was over the moon as I watched her dance on television wearing the gift my fan club had sent.

It must have been quite difficult for the Regulars to answer all of that mail. The cost of postage alone, not to mention the time and effort to get all of that information out and the letters written, must have been remarkable. I understood that some of the Regulars had families who helped them, but many sent out their own information sheets. We would write back to the fans, sending updated news and snapshots. It made us feel like we were a part of the show—a part of rock 'n' roll history.

In the late 1950s, Dick Clark began *Dick Clark's Saturday Night Beechnut Show*, featuring top singers like the Everly Brothers, Frankie Avalon, and Chuck Berry. Clark often brought a busload of Regulars with him from Philadelphia to sit in the audience. Teens in the audience screamed for the Regulars and treated them as though they were the stars performing.

Who could forget Jerry Lee Lewis, Mary Wells, Chubby Checker, and Buddy Holly? Who could stay in their seat when Little Richard sang about "Lucille," Danny and the Juniors told us "Rock and Roll is Here to Stay," or Elvis wanted you to be his "Teddy Bear"? With lyrics for teens, enjoyable melodies, and a beat to dance to, rock 'n' roll was everywhere, and *American Bandstand* brought it right into our living rooms.

When I think back to those days, I feel so incredibly fortunate to have lived during those years and experienced the excitement and colossal fun of the newness of rock 'n' roll. *American Bandstand* and the Regular dancers were a huge part of that era; what wonderful memories—memories never to be forgotten.

Stephanie Hammonds *(aka Steffi Welch) has been a rock 'n' roll and* American Bandstand *fan since the show first broadcast from Philadelphia on 1950s black-and-white television. Stephanie is still in touch with many of the Regulars she knew from the late 1950s through the early 1960s.*

Arlene Sullivan and Mary Ann Cuff.

Stephanie Hammonds.

John DeMarco, Arlene Sullivan's International Fan Club President

John DeMarco was the International Fan Club President for Arlene Sullivan. He also had a huge crush on her. For his fan club, John had his own newsletter, monthly brochures, an official card, and an Arlene Sullivan photograph.

John went to *American Bandstand* every Friday from age 14 until age 17; he danced on the Clay Cole Show from Monday to Thursday. John's Friday trip from Sheepshead Bay, Brooklyn, to Philadelphia took several hours.

In the late 1950s and early 1960s, John would invite a bunch of Regulars to come up to Brooklyn to attend weekend sock hops and church dances. They included Arlene, Pat Molittieri, Ivette and Carmen Jimenez, Jimmy Peatross, Joan Buck, Frank Brancaccio, Bill Cook, and Myrna Horowitz.

John DeMarco, President of Arlene Sullivan's International Fan Club, with Arlene.

'*Teen Magazine* featured six cover stories about the *American Bandstand* Regulars between 1958 and 1960, plus issued two 80-page Special Issues. The Regulars were treated just like the famous Hollywood actors and actresses in many top celebrity magazines.

Visiting Arlene Sullivan

BY JEAN BUTTZ

The year was 1958, and I was in the eighth grade. Every day at lunch, all of my friends were talking about a new show on television called *American Bandstand*. I decided that I needed to watch so I could be part of the conversation. My neighbor and best friend, Marilyn Thom, and I began watching *American Bandstand* every afternoon after school. We would hurry to be sure we were home by the time the show started. We learned the names of the Regulars who came to the show each day and began to look for fan clubs for our favorites so that we could learn more about each of them.

My parents and I always took a vacation in the summer and would decide our destination based on a family vacation planning meeting. Naturally, I began to lobby for a trip to Philadelphia. Since they knew how obsessed Marilyn and I were with watching *American Bandstand* every afternoon, they agreed that Philadelphia would indeed be our destination. I knew that my first trip to *American Bandstand* would be a significant entry on the timeline of my life.

It was Thursday, August 21, 1958, at 1:30 p.m. that I first arrived at WFIL studios. My parents had driven me all the way there from Illinois. I waited in a long line for what seemed like an eternity. All of a sudden, everyone started screaming. I asked the policeman standing beside me what had happened. He said Kenny Rossi had just arrived. It wasn't long until Kenny walked right past me. I took his picture. My hands were shaking because I could not believe I had just seen one of the Regulars. After that, I asked a man who was working there what kind of a chance I had to get into the show since there were so many people in front of me. He said, "I'd advise you to go home." I couldn't believe I had gotten this close and now I had to leave. Sadly, I headed for the parking lot to reunite with my parents.

In the meantime, my dad had struck up a conversation with the man in charge of the parking lot, telling him how excited I was and how far we had driven just so I could be on *American Bandstand*. Upon hearing my sad tale that I would not get into the show, that kind gentleman walked me to the front of the line and told the policeman to let me in. Soon the doors opened, and I was escorted into the studio along with so many other excited teenagers.

We were instructed to sit down. The producer, Tony Mammarella, said we were on the air. I was so disappointed because none of the Regulars were there yet. After the first song, they all came in; Arlene and Kenny were first. As soon as I saw them, I got up and went to talk to them, but the song had started and they were already dancing.

I had turned around to return to my seat when Justine came in. Right away I went over to talk to her. I told her where I was from and how much I liked watching her and Bob. I asked her why Bob had not been at the show for a while; she said that he had a summer job and was working, but as soon as school started again, he would be coming every day. After she had signed my autograph book, I thanked her and set out to find Arlene and Kenny.

Soon I located them and introduced myself. While Arlene was signing my autograph book, I explained that I had come all the way from Decatur, Illinois, just to see her and Kenny and the other Regulars. When she finished writing, she looked at me and said, "Well, are you disappointed?" I explained that I could never be disappointed and that my friends and I watched the show every afternoon and talked about it at lunch every day. She shook her head in disbelief and winked at me. During several other dances, she smiled as she and Kenny danced past me.

Before I knew it, it was time for a spotlight dance. I was standing by the top ten board when suddenly someone came up behind me and put their arm around my waist. I could not imagine who it would be, but when I turned around it was Arlene. She stood there for the rest of the dance talking to me with Kenny right behind her. During the show, I was able to dance with Arlene, Kenny, Justine, Peggy Leonard, Mary and Rosalie Beltrante, and Barb Levick. Before I knew it, the doors were opening again and it was time to leave. I waited outside to get some pictures of the Regulars as they left.

All of a sudden, I saw Arlene again. I went over to thank her for being so nice. She said, "Don't forget me. Write and send me a picture, OK?" I responded that I would, but I did not have her address. To my amazement, she wrote her home address on a piece of paper and handed it to me. As I walked away, it felt like I was dreaming. I had actually been on *American Bandstand* that day, met my favorite Regulars, danced with some of

drove us back to the motel. Arlene and I had enjoyed a quiet night of conversation, picture taking, and listening to records. Our parents had also enjoyed getting to know each other. I am still amazed to this day how gracious and welcoming that family always was to us and others who just showed up expecting to spend time with them. I am sure Arlene would have rather been doing something with her friends instead of entertaining me, but she made me feel like I was the most important person around any time I was with her.

I was heading into my senior year of high school, and with Arlene working and no longer on *American Bandstand*, I knew it would probably be the last time I would see her. That made the time we spent together even more special. That night was a perfect way to end the many years she and her family had made my life so special. I was thrilled to reconnect with her on Facebook a few years ago, and I look forward to seeing her again someday.

Arlene Sullivan's #1 Fans

Jean Buttz and Marilyn Donovan then (notice the cute bows in their hair).

Jean Buttz and Marilyn Donovan now.

Jean Haher Buttz and Marilyn Thom Donovan watched *American Bandstand* together every afternoon they didn't have after-school activities. If neither was able to watch the show, they had one of their mothers do the honors. They kept a daily notebook which included: whether Arlene and Kenny danced on the show that day; how many songs the couple danced together; what outfit Arlene was wearing; and anything else that might have happened during the show. They also wrote out a list of songs that were played on the show that day. They started this diary in 1959, on Arlene's 16th birthday. They continued it for two years.

Since the show was in black-and-white, the duo imagined what colors each of Arlene's outfits might have been. They also noted when Arlene and Kenny danced with other Regulars, and imagined reasons why they weren't together for those dances. Since their school classmates discussed *American Bandstand* during the lunch period, they would ask Jean and Marilyn to fill in any details about the previous day's show.

Their devotion to Arlene extended into their selection of outfits to buy for themselves. When they went shopping together, the two tried to buy similar skirts and blouses to the clothes Arlene wore on television. "We found out later that those rounded collars many Regulars wore were part of their Catholic school uniforms," Jean remembers.

"We called Arlene every few months, and wrote her regularly," Marilyn said. She remembers that they would make a list of questions about things they wondered about from their diary notes. "Arlene would then clarify what really happened or why she had not been at the show on a particular day," Marilyn added.

On special occasions like Arlene's birthday, Christmas shows, or anniversary shows, they recorded the program on a tape recorder and later transcribed it word for word so they could re-read the notes frequently.

Marilyn recalled that her father would set up his photographic equipment when they got new photos of Arlene. Then they would expose the picture on a piece of photographic paper. When they moved the picture into the developing pan, they had "such fun watching Arlene appear onto the plain paper," Marilyn said.

When they visited Arlene in Philadelphia, Arlene looked at the diary and her response was "This is amazing, but you guys are nuts." Arlene's parents were also amazed that anyone would take the time to keep track of every detail of *American Bandstand*.

"It was a labor of love, and it is fun to look back on even today," Jean reminisced.

The Honorary American Bandstand Regular

Growing up in the 1950s, 15-year-old Joel Diamond had a teenage obsession for *American Bandstand* and especially Arlene Sullivan.

In 1985, Diamond headed up Sony/April Blackwood Music, working with many big recording artists. He was living beyond his wildest dreams in a penthouse apartment on Central Park South in Manhattan. Through business colleagues, he met Arlene and took her to dinner one evening.

One month later, Joel invited Arlene, Kenny Rossi, Frankie Lobis, and Betty Romantini to his apartment for a gourmet meal. Joel was in seventh heaven. And right before leaving, Arlene said to him, "Joel, we have agreed that if we had known you back then, you would have been one of us." They presented Joel with a gift he treasures to this day. It is a trophy that sits on top of his piano and is engraved with the inscription: *To Joel Diamond, Honorary American Bandstand Regular.*

Joel Diamond's prized possession—his trophy from the *American Bandstand* Regulars.

Joel Diamond and his dinner guests: Arlene, Kenny, Betty Romantini, and Frankie Lobis.

David Frees, American Bandstand's #1 FAN

Davey "Pop Frosty" Frees definitely deserves his place in *American Bandstand* history—even though he never set foot in the studio while the show was broadcast from Philadelphia. Although his parents wouldn't let him take the train in from the suburbs, he's made up for the lost opportunity as the founder and president of the *American Bandstand* Fan Club.

Davey's fascination for the show began when he was just five years old, as he watched the dancers on Bob Horn's *Bandstand* and danced with his refrigerator door. His mom, Ethel, encouraged Davey to watch the show, and it became his part-time baby-sitter. He continued to watch the show when it became Dick Clark's *American Bandstand* until it finally went off the air in 1989. "I never stopped watching the show," Davey said, "It was a cure for a bad day; it taught us to dance and it made us smile."

Davey became president of an existing fan club for Carmen and Ivette Jimenez in 1960, when he was 13 years old. He also was working on an *American Bandstand* fan club, but when the teenage presidents stopped having fan clubs when the show moved to California in 1964, he dropped the group temporarily. Unfortunately, Davey lost thousands of photos when there was a flood in his attic in 1968.

After Davey returned from a tour in Vietnam, he decided to turn the fan club into a memory club to honor the whole *American Bandstand* history and its nostalgia. It initially was free as members would send in a stamped self-addressed envelope. Many fan club presidents sold him their photographs. Then Dick Clark approved the *American Bandstand* Fan Club in 1970, and Davey became the president, a role he's enjoyed for over 45 years.

He fondly remembers writing letters to the Regulars. "We would send a self-addressed envelope with our fan letters and many would write back," Davey said. "It was a magical day when you received a letter back!" He told the *New York Times* that he lived out "in the sticks with cows and stuff, and there wasn't much," and when he watched the show it "was like a whole set of friends when you came home from school."

He counts many lasting friendships with the Regulars, including Carmen and Ivette Jimenez, Eddie Kelly, Jim Hudson, Barbara Marcen, Arlene Sullivan, and Kenny

Rossi. His one regret is that he never met Frani Giordano.

Davey lives about 150 miles from Philadelphia. He has a daughter, Michelle, named for Michelle Leibowitz. His partner, David Hill, helps him run the *American Bandstand* Fan Club. And he still dances, not with his refrigerator door, but with local dancers on the monthly *BCTV Dance Party* in Reading, Pennsylvania.

Davey still receives handwritten notes from Kari Clark whenever he mails her the annual *Bandstand Boogies* newsletter. He deserves the title of *American Bandstand*'s #1 fan for his devotion to preserving *American Bandstand* history for so many years.

For membership in the *American Bandstand* Fan Club, the lifetime membership fee is $10. Please send a check payable to Davey Frees, 52 Stauffer Park Lane, Mohnton, PA, 19540.

Davey with Carmen and Ivette.

Davey with Pop Singer.

Davey with Ronnie Caldora and Myrna Horowitz.

Davey with Myrna Horowitz and Marci Fishman at Dick Clark's Grill.

Davey with Carmen Jimenez.

Davey with Carmen and partner, David Hill.

Davey with JoAnn Franchi.

Davey with a fan in his *Bandstand* bedroom.

Davey in his *Bandstand* bedroom.

American Bandstand Visit, July 4, 1960

BY DON GILLIS

In July of 1960, when I was a teen, I watched AB every day. I also was on a local dance party, called *The Jack Spector Show*, where I met Lydia Beben, who was the president of Kenny Rossi's Fan Club. We met every Saturday for the local show which was on from 3 to 5 p.m. on WPRO-TV in Providence, RI.

I never thought I would ever get to visit Dick Clark's *American Bandstand*, but one day Lydia and I were talking about AB, and she said that her father and mother said that they were going to Philadelphia to visit and she asked me if I would like to come along with her, and her girlfriend Pat Stowell. I asked my parents if I could go, and they said I could.

So, on July 3, Mr. and Mrs. Beben picked me up at my home in Rhode Island, and we set out for the eight-hour drive. At that time the Connecticut turnpike had all the tolls, so it was a *long* ride, and very, very *hot*. We finally reached our destination and stayed at the Ben Franklin Hotel, in downtown Philly.

On the next morning, Lydia had set up an appointment to visit her idol, Kenny Rossi, who lived not too far from downtown, as I recall. Kenny was in his recording career at that time, and had been off the show for some time. He met us with open arms, and he, his father, and one of his brothers met with us, and we chatted on the steps to his house, then went inside for a bit. He was very nice, and his father and brothers were so cordial. Kenny's dad was a tailor, and they lived in one of the row houses (I had never seen one of those before). The meeting lasted until lunch time, when Kenny, who had just got a brand new red automobile, said he had some errands and wanted to get going. He left us with a smile and great memories.

If my memory serves me correctly, we went to lunch, and then to Market Street to the WFIL Studio where AB was broadcast. There was a long line at the outside, but Lydia had tickets for us, and we had no problem getting into the studio.

The Studio: WOW! I felt like I went into Never, Never Land. I was like a kid in a candy shop! My first thought as I looked around was how small the studio actually was, as it looked so much bigger on TV. It was very crowded, and I saw the three huge cameras sliding around and the infamous white line that you could not go over. The cameramen really had a tough time, as most of the kids overstepped the line.

***Bandstand* Time:** It hit me…I was *on American Bandstand*!! Dick Clark was at the podium, and I was talking with Lydia and Pat when I spotted Carmen Jimenez and Barbara Levick. I finally got to each of them individually to say hello and I asked them both if I could dance with them. As it turned out, it was dance fever week for the annual dance contest, and both of them would only dance with their dance partners in the contest. Thus, I was out of luck, but they were very gracious and friendly. I saw Carol Scaldeferri and Ivette Jimenez, I remember, and some other Regulars that were popular at the time. After 50 years, it's hard to recall every detail, but I do know that the guests were Buddy Knox and Jimmy Charles who sang "A Million To One." We all went to the autograph table after and I still have those autographs.

Meeting Dick Clark: I finally got up the nerve to go to the podium to get a closer look and ask for Dick's autograph. He was much smaller than I thought, and he wore a lot of makeup. He was just as you saw him on TV, but he controlled those kids with an iron fist. He had a telephone on the podium desk, and it was used as an intercom system, which he would use to move the kids around, such as telling them to get back from the front line cameras if he thought they were there too long. He definitely ran that show. I went away with his autograph, and a completely different picture of him in my mind. He just surprised me, especially when he was on that telephone.

Fast Forward: Well, the studio time had expired and it was time to leave. I remember getting a lump in my throat because I wanted to stay! We exited in groups out the back door, which led to a parking lot. It was a beautiful day in Philly, and the fresh air smelled great after being in the very warm crowded studio.

Memory Lane: I have some pictures that I took after the show, outside the studio, of Carmen and me, Ivette and Carmen, Barbara Levick and me, Lydia and me, and Pat Stowell. It was great taking and now having those pictures because they are one of a kind.

Don Gillis with Kenny Rossi.

Don Gillis and Lydia Beben with Kenny Rossi and his family.

The Early 1960s on American Bandstand

BY RICK FISHER

As a child, I enjoyed watching *American Bandstand* several times a week, starting during the Bob Horn years, but I really got into it in 1957. I lived in a neighborhood where all of the kids danced and we learned the new dances from our idols, the Regulars. I watched often enough to become familiar with the kids; it really was like watching a reality show. We knew all of their names, and bit by bit, their lives were revealed to us. We looked for our favorites each day and if they weren't there, we were concerned.

In 1959, the Regulars started to appear in *Teen* and *16* magazines and the missing pieces were unveiled. They became like stars and I knew that I would *have* to attend the show.

Rick Fisher and Ann Marie Maslan.

You were supposed to be fourteen years old to attend, but in March 1961, at age thirteen, I decided to show up. I took my girlfriend, Sharon Pinkenson, with me, who was only twelve. After taking a bus and the el, we arrived at 46th and Market Streets at 1 p.m. We got in line and hoped for the best. We were in different lines, as they were separated by gender. Sharon was all made up so that she looked old enough to get in. I looked about ten, but Bob the Cop let us both in.

While we were waiting, I chatted with the other guys. At about 3 p.m., the Regulars started parading up the street. It was like being in Hollywood. This was during the finals of the Pony Contest, and the Regulars were all there. I can see it like it was yesterday. The first Regular I saw was Judy Leibowitz, and I nearly fell over when I saw the cigarette in her hand. For the next ten minutes, several more walked by and were let right in.

The next thing that I knew, the line was moving and I got in. I met Sharon in the hall and we walked into the studio. It was so different from what I had expected—much smaller and somewhat tattered looking. They sat us in the bleachers and all I could do was stare at my idols. They were all there: Frani Giordano, Mike Balara, Barbara Levick, Carole Scaldeferri, Flossie Harvey, Louie Lucas, Arlene DiPietro, Mary and Susie Beltrante, Betty Romantini, Jay Jacovini, Mary Burns, Frank Ruggerio, Steve Colanero, Joyce Shafer, Norman Kerr, Ed Kelly, Monte Montes, Frankie Vacca, Marlyn Brown, Diane Iaquinto, Charlie Hibib, and several more. As much as they excited me, the love of my life was there—Carmen Jimenez. Once I saw her, my life was complete.

Sharon and I danced every dance, and I managed to maneuver myself next to Carmen as often as possible. I even ended up sitting next to her while Clarence Frogman Henry was performing "(I Don't Know Why) But I Do." I was too intimidated to speak to her, but just being next to her was total heaven on earth.

I left totally elated and knew that I would return. Between that day and June 1963, I was on about fifty shows. Some were live and some were on tape, so I actually got to watch myself at home when the show was aired. I became friendly with some of the Regulars in late 1962 and 1963. A few were at my home for a party, and I was at their homes, too. I was in the spotlight dances, was part of the record review (mathematician), and was selected to dance behind the map before and after the show. I felt like hot stuff.

I lost interest when the show moved to California, but when I met Carole Scaldeferri in 1991, we instantly hit it off and my interest was resurrected with a vengeance. I remained close with Carole and her husband Richard for twenty-three years, until her untimely death in 2013. I had a nice friendship with Carmella Astrella, too. There are several others whom I see or speak to irregularly. I was blessed to have lunch with Arlene Sullivan this past summer, along with Terri Cellie and her husband Lou DeNoble (Tommy's brother).

I stay in touch with them today. I have loved *American Bandstand* my entire life and love when I see and speak to those whom I loved from the show.

Philadelphia Through the Eyes of a Stranger

BY MARLENE MIZANIN

I've written many articles about my adventures in Philadelphia, but one thing I never write about is my very first trip to the city and my experience on *American Bandstand*. I was just like one million other teens in this country. Every day I would rush home from school to see my favorite Regulars, and every day I would long for a time when I could meet them. To me, they were exceptional teens who were different from all of the rest of us. Needless to say, that notion proved entirely wrong.

I started writing to a Regular named Betty Romantini (now Mrs. Natale). Betty and I became close friends through the mail and after writing to her for almost a year, I finally talked my parents into taking me and my girlfriend, Joanne, to the City of Brotherly Love. I had read stories about the Regulars being snobs, and was shaking like a leaf when I walked into Pop Singer's. I went up to Pop and told him I was from Chicago. Within five minutes, he was hugging and kissing me and Joanne.

Soon, the Regulars began coming in to socialize before the show. Pop brought all the kids over to our table. Louie Lucas, Flossie Harvey, Mike Balara, Mary Brown, Diane Iaquinto, Frankie Vacca, Joanne Hall, Ronnie Caldora, Joyce Shafer and Norman Kerr, Judy and Michele Leibowitz, Thom Cardwell, JoAnn Franchi, Monte Montes, and Arlene and Bob DiPietro were just a small number of the Regulars I met. Finally, Betty came in and she acted as if I were her own sister. She hugged me and said how glad she was that I could come. Joanne and I sat down and were pulled in with the rest of the crowd. I was like one of them.

When it was time to go to the studio, Betty took us in and introduced me to all of the personnel at WFIL. She even introduced me to Dick Clark and Charlie O'Donnell. Once it was time to start dancing, Joanne and I had thought we would end up spending an hour and a half on the benches as onlookers. Our time was quite different from what we expected.

The music started and Monte and Frankie Vacca came up to Joanne and me and asked us to dance. We were shocked, to say the least. After we danced with them, Thom Cardwell and Norm asked us to double dance with Carolyn De Simine and Joyce Shafer. Much to our surprise, Joanne and I danced almost every dance that afternoon. It was then that I knew we were all the same teens.

After the show, it was time to go back to Pop's. When we all rushed in, Pop ran up to me and said that there was someone he wanted us to meet. From our conversation before the show, he knew that I adored Freddy Cannon. There in their glory were Freddy's mother and sister. Pop introduced me to them and that was the beginning of our close friendship now. I also met Carmen at the time.

Marlene Mizanin with Jerry Blavat.

She was already barred from the show, so she only came to Pop's to see Mrs. Cannon and Mary Lou.

When we left, all of the Regulars told us to be sure to make it to the show the next day. We came back the following day and met the same group, along with Bob Kelly, Ed Kelly, Carole Persiani, Steve Lewis, Richie Cartledge, and Paula Kopicko. The same thing happened that day as well—we had a marvelous time.

After the show, I met Myrna Horowitz, and she actually invited me to stay at her house. Little did I know that the following Christmas I would stay with her family. Myrna later came to Chicago and stayed with me.

That was just the beginning of my many trips to Philadelphia. No matter what anyone may say to me, Philadelphia through the eyes of a stranger is fabulous. There are no words that can really describe the City of Brotherly Love.

American Bandstand fans frequently took photographs of their favorite Regulars dancing with their cameras. Sometimes they would mail a screenshot to a Regular to get an autograph.

The Best of Bandstand

Chapter 10

Backstage Bandstand

One of the most watched *American Bandstand* broadcasts aired on December 5, 1961. It was a special show called "Backstage Bandstand" and Dick gave a shout out to all the crew members, stage hands, cameramen, and the director, Ed Yates.

American Bandstand fans got to watch the studio actually being set up for the daily show by the dedicated and fast-moving crew.

Ed Yates, director, in the Control Room.

Musical Bandstand

One of *American Bandstand's* legacies is the introduction of the artists who created or rose to stardom in the years when rock 'n' roll was just entering the mainstream of American pop music. In the 1950s, Philadelphia was the epicenter of rock 'n' roll. It was a tryout town; new songs were released daily, and, depending on their popularity, they were either released nationwide or relegated to local markets. *American Bandstand* was the perfect venue to introduce the new music; viewers across the country heard the songs at the same time—this was new; and the young audience in the studio and at home was the perfect group to judge the music.

When Bob Horn's *Bandstand* hit the airways, the sound of music was still calm and geared to older Americans. It was more 1940s than 1950s; decades always linger until the middle of the following one. Horn played host to many of the performers of the day, including Patti Page, Frankie Laine, Joni James, Johnny Ray, Julius La Rosa, and Philadelphian Eddie Fisher. Ballads prevailed. By the time *American Bandstand* hit the national airwaves in 1957, the musical lineup was changing drastically.

Primary among the new talent were a plethora of Philadelphians. Bill Haley and His Comets catapulted the new music into the American psyche with "(We're Gonna) Rock Around The Clock"; although they had had earlier hits, this one helped define rock 'n' roll. Charlie Gracie had what some consider one of the first rock 'n' roll songs recorded, "Boogie Woogie Blues," in 1951; but he introduced his "Butterfly" on the show and it became an instant million seller (three million to be exact). Lee

Andrews and the Hearts from Bartram High School in Southwest Philadelphia had a hit with "Long, Long and Lonely Nights" in 1957. They followed with two more national hits, "Teardrops" and "Try the Impossible." Striking it big was another group from Bartram High School, Danny and the Juniors. The four guys struck gold when Dick Clark suggested they rename their record "At the Hop" instead of "Let's All Do the Bop." The group scored again with "Rock and Roll Is Here to Stay."

Because *American Bandstand* featured at least ten acts a week, it was necessary to have fall-back performers who could make it to the studio at a moment's notice. Dick relied on some talented good-looking young men from South Philadelphia; they quickly became the show's "Teen Idols"; they were Frankie Avalon ("De De Dinah"), James Darren ("Goodbye Cruel World"), Fabian ("I'm A Man"), and Bobby Rydell ("Kissin' Time"). They all lived near the studio and it served them well. Of course, the fifth singer from South Philadelphia to skyrocket to fame on *American Bandstand* was Chubby Checker, with a series of hits including, the game-changer, "The Twist," and later "Pony Time."

Other Philadelphians introduced on *American Bandstand* were: Jodie Sands ("With All My Heart"), Dee Dee Sharp ("Mashed Potato Time"), Patti LaBelle, also from Bartram High School, singing with the Bluebelles ("I Sold My Heart to the Junkman"), Bill Doggett ("Honky-Tonk"), The Dovells ("The Bristol Stomp"), The Orlons ("Wah Watusi"), The Silhouettes ("Get A Job"), and Mike Pedicin ("Shake a Hand").

Of course, the show was not just Philadelphians singing; many others got their start or shot to fame after an appearance on the show in those early years. Among them were: Paul Anka ("Diana"), Connie Francis ("Who's Sorry Now"), Jimmie Rodgers ("Honeycomb"), The Delvikings ("Come Go With Me"), Billy and Lillie ("La Dee Dah"), Dion and the Belmonts ("No One Knows"), The Champs ("Tequila"), Eddie Cochran ("Summertime Blues"), Bobby Helms ("Jingle Bell Rock"), Frankie Ford ("Sea Cruise"), Freddy Cannon ("Tallahassee Lassie"), The Drifters ("There Goes My Baby"), Duane Eddy ("Lotta Lovin'"), Jerry Lee Lewis ("Whole Lotta Shakin Going On"), Dale Hawkins ("Susie Q"), the Everly Brothers ("Wake Up Little Susie"), Jackie Wilson ("Reet Petite"), The Crickets ("That'll Be The Day"), and Thurston Harris ("Little Bitty Pretty One").

There's no question that without *American Bandstand*, rock 'n' roll might have been nothing more than a passing fad; or it might have taken much longer to establish itself as a genuine musical genre. Dick Clark called the music of *American Bandstand* the soundtrack of our lives. For those of us who tuned every day to watch the show, the music remains exactly that.

The Day the Music Didn't Die

Buddy Holly, Ritchie Valens, and J.P. Richardson ("The Big Bopper") all appeared on *American Bandstand* and all three made significant contributions to music as rock and roll pioneers. There are many things to be said of their gifts! Buddy's songwriting, his invention of the modern rock band (lead guitar, drums, and bass), and the fact that he and The Crickets were the first band to write, perform, and produce their own songs are a few noteworthy points. Ritchie Valens opened doors for Chicano rock, but most importantly, he was the first ethnic artist to cross-over into popular music with his hit song "La Bamba." "The Big Bopper" also created the music video genre long before MTV came on the scene.

Since 1979, rock 'n' roll fans, called the "February Family" have traveled from across the world to make the pilgrimage to Clear Lake, Iowa, and the Surf Ballroom, where Holly, Valens, and Richardson gave their final career performance on February 2, 1959. Their airplane crashed a short time after the concert just five miles from the Surf Ballroom.

Twin sisters Sheryl Davis (right) and Sherry Davis (left) pose with the Buddy Holly glasses sculpture at the gateway to the memorial (crash) site Saturday, February 6, 2016 (see photo). This gateway marks the ¼-mile walk to where the plane came to rest just after 1 a.m. on Feb. 3, 1959. The Davis twins are music heritage preservationists and created an historical record of the 2016 Winter Dance Party through the eyes of the "February Family" with their new research initiative, *The Surf Speaks: Voices of a Living History* (www.thesurfspeaks.com).

Buddy Holly at the Surf Ballroom, February 2, 1959.
Richie Valens at the Surf Ballroom, February 2, 1959.
Sheryl and Sherry Davis at the gateway to the Memorial Site.
The "February Family" at the Surf Ballroom, February 2, 2016.

1957 Winners for *American Bandstand*'s Annual Music Poll

- Patti Page – Favorite Female Vocalist
- Elvis Presley – Favorite Male Vocalist
- Rick Nelson – Most Promising New Male Vocalist
- Janice Harper – Most Promising New Female Vocalist
- Jerry Lee Lewis – Best Instrumental Combo
- Danny and The Juniors – Best Vocal Group
- "All Shook Up" - Best Record by Elvis Presley

Singers and Album Covers

Some of the singers who performed on *American Bandstand*... Most of these photos are from recent reunions and anniversary parties.

Dancing Bandstand

Dancing for Prizes

One of the easiest ways to keep the public involved in a TV show is to let viewers interact with it. Dick Clark knew this back in the 1950s, and he knew that the easiest way to involve the home viewers in *American Bandstand* was to hold an annual dance contest and let the viewers pick the winners. To make it interesting, the contests always featured a different dance, and if you won first prize, you were ineligible the following year. Dance contests were familiar to most Americans in the 1950s. Schools, churches, and neighborhood clubs held them all the time. Even neighborhood block parties often ended with a dance contest.

On *American Bandstand*, the contestants wore large black numbers on their backs. Viewers sent in post cards listing the number of the couple they preferred. The contests proved Dick's point about the viewers was right; almost a million post cards were delivered to the studio during the contest weeks.

So who won the contests? Arlene and Kenny won strange little Italian cars when they won the Cha-Cha contest; Frani Giordano and Mike Balara also won cars dancing the Pony. Justine and Bob jitterbugged their way to first place and new jukeboxes filled with two hundred records. Dottie Horner and Frankie Spagnuola took first place in the Chalypso contest (a dance created on the show); they won portable TV sets. Pat Molittieri and Billy Cook won in-ground swimming pools for slow dancing. Jimmy Peatross and Joan Buck took first prize doing what they did as well as the strand, the jitterbug. They, too, won cars. The irony was that many of the kids who won cars were still too young to drive. Like most contests, the *American Bandstand* results had more to do with popularity than with talent. The winners of these contests were always the show's most popular Regulars.

A definitive list of winners is impossible as time and some fans' memories don't always "jive" with each other

Bandstand Dance Contest Winners

1957—Chalypso Contest

"Little Darlin'," by The Diamonds

1st Place: Dottie Horner and Frank Spagnuola—Portable Television Set Prize
2nd Place: Charlette Russo and Michael (Delfatti) DeLano
3rd Place: Lynn Boehmer and Jack Diamond

1957—Jitterbug Contest

"Rock and Roll Music," by Chuck Berry

1st Place: Justine Carrelli and Bob Clayton—Jukebox Prize
2nd Place: Dottie Horner and Frank Spagnuola
3rd Place: Unknown

1958—Cha Cha Contest

"La Dah, La Dah," by Billy and Lillie

1st Place: Arlene Sullivan and Kenny Rossi—Isetta 300 (Italian car) Prize
2nd Place: Dottie Horner and Larry Giuliani
3rd Place: Joanne MonteCarlo and Frank Lobis

1958—Slow Dance

"The End," by Earl Grant

1st Place: Pat Molittieri and Billy Cook—Swimming Pool Prize
2nd Place: Barbara Levick and Walt Grzelak
3rd Place: Janet Hamill and Tex Connor

1959—Jitterbug Contest

"Tallahassee Lassie," by Freddy Cannon

1st Place: Joan Buck and Jimmy Peatross—Simca (car) Prize
2nd Place: Janet Hamill and Tex Connor
3rd Place: Barbara Levick and Joe Wissert

1960—Jitterbug Contest

"Finger Poppin' Time," by Hank Ballard

1st Place: Barbara Levick and Billy Cook—Prize of Three Televisions
2nd Place: Arlene DiPietro and Billy Young
3rd Place: Carmen Jimenez and Bob Kelly

1961—Pony Contest

"Pony Train," by The Conductor

1st Prize: Frani Giordano and Mike Bolara—Ford Convertible Prize
2nd Place: Joyce Shafer and Norman Kerr
3rd Place: Carmen Jimenez and Frank Vacca

1962—Mashed Potato Contest

"Mashed Potato Time," by Dee Dee Sharp

1st Place: Paula Kopicko and Richie Cartledge—Motorboat Prize
2nd Place: Marlyn Brown and Frank Vacca
3rd Place: Diane Iaquinto and Charlie Hibib

The Dances

The Regulars danced their way into our hearts on *American Bandstand*. Remember these dances from your black-and-white screen?

- Slow Dance
- Hand Jive
- Hully Gully
- The Bop
- The Stroll
- The Pony
- The Twist
- The Fly
- Circle Dance
- Double Dance
- The Jerk
- Chalypso—Calypso + Cha-Cha
- The Mashed Potato
- Bristol Stomp
- The Slop
- The Strand
- The Locomotion
- Jitterbug
- The Walk
- The Watusi

Announcing the Dance Contest Winners

BY BARBARA GILSTRAP

I was obsessed with *American Bandstand* when I was a teenager and rushed home from school every day to watch it. Dancing with the door, I taught myself a reasonable facsimile of the fast dance steps I saw the Regulars do.

My enthusiasm peaked at dance contest time. This particular year the contest winners were going to be announced in the spring—a time of frequent electrical storms, and sometimes even tornados, in East Texas where I lived. My mother's greatest fear was that the television antenna would attract lightening and burn out the TV, if not burn down the house. Her rule was that the TV was to be turned off and unplugged if there was any hint of an electrical storm. Before she left for work that morning, she listened to the weather forecast and informed me that storms were predicted later in the day. "Do not turn on the television today," she warned me. *But this is the day the dance contest winners are announced*, I thought!

By the time I got home from school the sky had begun to darken and turn an eerie green. There was no thunder or lightning yet, so I turned on the television. Dick Clark told us to stay tuned for the announcement of the dance contest winners as they went to commercial break. The picture on the TV jumped, and I heard some crackling. I turned off the TV for a minute or so. The sky was darker and greener, and there was a buzz in the air. However, this was probably the moment of the announcement, so, holding my breath, I turned the TV back on. I could see that the contestants were still standing around Dick Clark, so no announcement had been made. Thank goodness!

Just then a bolt of lightning ripped across the sky and into the large old chinaberry tree that overhung our house. The tree crashed onto our roof with a sound loud enough to rival the thunder then booming around me. My heart leapt out of my chest and somewhere up into my throat area, making breathing difficult. However, I noted that the television miraculously was still working. Just as I was counting my blessings, my mother returned from work and saw the tree lying on her house. She dashed from the car through the sheets of rain that had now started and cleared the front door shrieking. "Barbara, what in the world—"

"Shh!" I said, interrupting her, "They're announcing the dance contest winners!"

TV Bandstand

Author Fran Priddy dedicated *TV Bandstand* to Pat Molittieri because she was the inspiration for the main character, Sue Kelsey, and the plot of the book. Fran also thanked Dick Clark and the other *Bandstand* Regulars who influenced the story line.

Commercial Bandstand

American Bandstand's popularity extended into many collectables that fans purchased, including Dick Clark dolls, autograph books, record carry cases, paper dolls, fashions, and stuffed animals. There were even *American Bandstand* Dancing Shoes that retailed for $8.95, but were later discounted to $5 by some shoe stores.

Believe It or Not Bandstand

- When *American Bandstand* debuted on ABC, the show had no sponsors, so ABC picked up the tab to pay for the broadcast.
- The acne medicine Clearasil was one of the first *American Bandstand* sponsors. It helped that the ABC President lived next door to the owner of this company.
- Dick Clark stood on two telephone books to kiss Victoria Shaw in *Because They're Young*.
- In 1962 Bobby Vee sang "Please don't ask about Barbara." Dick Clark wouldn't play it on *American Bandstand* because he was divorcing his wife named Barbara at the time.
- Actress Peggy Lipton was a president of the Mike Balara fan club.
- Dick Clark and his wife Kari were married on 7/7/77 in a ceremony that started at 7 p.m. His address in Burbank at that time was P.O. Box 7777.
- America's first baby boomer, Kathleen Casey Kirschling (born 1 second after midnight, January 1, 1946), danced on *American Bandstand*, her favorite show, as a teenager. She would throw a sweater over her Catholic school uniform and take the bus to the studio.

  "I had a hot-pink Hula Hoop, which I loved. I also wore mohair sweaters, wore my hair teased up in a bubble, and I thought about joining the Peace Corps," she told *People Magazine* (January 8, 1996).
- Ron Joseph was given Dick Clark's original Top Ten Board from 1958 to use on his television show. RJ was the only *American Bandstand* Regular to have his own television show like Dick Clark's show.
- *American Bandstand* Shoes "were being advertised to black teenagers in the *Philadelphia Tribune* at the same time black teenagers were being turned away from the show's studio audience."—Matt Delmont, author, *The Nicest Kids on the Block*
- The cameramen shooting *American Bandstand* took special aim—frequently shooting the Regulars' faces as they danced cheek to cheek or following their foot work to the latest dance steps.

An American Bandstand Romance

Joyce Berman was a Regular on *American Bandstand* between 1958 and 1961, traveling from her Northeast Philadelphia home to the studio at least four times weekly. Her passion was dancing and she often danced with Harvey Robbins, Bobby DiPietro, and Fran Hardman.

A dapper young gentleman, Eddie Mills, came to the show from Brooklyn one afternoon in 1959, hopefully to meet and dance with Carole Scaldeferri. Carole didn't attend the show that day, but Joyce, 15, noticed Eddie sitting alone and asked him to slow dance a Ladies' Choice.

They did keep in contact between Philadelphia and Brooklyn after that first meeting, and occasionally saw each other when she traveled to the Bronx to see her grandmother. But something magical clicked because the two were married five years later, when Joyce was 20. They were married for 52 years until Eddie passed away in 2016. Joyce Berman is now Dr. Joyce Mills, a nationally known psychotherapist and author.

Mystery Bandstand

Reruns

One of the most frequently asked questions by *American Bandstand* fans is, "Will we ever be able to see videos of the show during its Philadelphia years?" Popular TV shows broadcast between 1956 and 1964 can be seen regularly on cable or YouTube, why not *American Bandstand*? The answer lies in a technical recording called a kinescope.

A kinescope is a motion picture filmed off a television screen. The lead cameraman on *Bandstand* usually handled the transfers from a studio monitor. The quality was never pristine and often washed out; but it was the only way to preserve a live show for later broadcast in those years before videotape. George Yates, whose father was *American Bandstand*'s director, says *Bandstand* used three cameras to capture the five-days-a-week, two-and-a-half-hours-a-day show. That amounted to hundreds of shows a year. According to Yates, "Hardy any of those shows were recorded as kinescopes because it was just too expensive." And, because the film stock was so expensive, what kinescopes were made, were often reused, erasing any recording on them.

Yates believes there are probably a couple dozen *American Bandstand* kinescopes of the Philadelphia years in existence, but these are probably recordings of special shows like the Christmas shows or picnic shows. He believes Dick Clark Productions has some in its archives, but has not released them. Private collectors may have bought up others that exist, and are holding them from the public.

So, to answer *Bandstand* fans, the likelihood of seeing more than a few segments of the old shows is highly unlikely.

policies because they feared that racial tensions around the studio in West Philadelphia would alienate advertisers.

Rather than a strict whites-only policy (like at Baltimore's *Buddy Deane Show*, made famous in John Waters' *Hairspray*), *Bandstand* used other means to block black teens from the studio. In addition to a dress code, Clark's show required visitors to write in advance to request tickets, and these applications were screened by name and address. Black teenagers undermined this ticket plan on at least one occasion. "I engineered a plan to get membership applications," Walter Palmer told me, "and gave them Irish, Polish, and Italian last names. They mailed the forms back to our homes, and once we had the cards, we were able to get in that day."

Despite this, Clark claimed for years that he integrated *Bandstand* by the late 1950s. He first commented on the program's integration in his 1976 autobiography, when *American Bandstand*'s ratings were in decline and the show faced a challenge from Don Cornelius's *Soul Train*. When Clark initially referred to *American Bandstand*'s "integration," he emphasized black musical artists performing on the show. From 1976 to 2011, however, Clark became progressively bolder, and less accurate, in his retelling of how he integrated the studio audience.

We often use the history of popular culture to talk about the history of race in America. We don't want to remember all-American *American Bandstand* as discriminating against black teenagers. And that says more about our desire to embrace a more comforting narrative of racial progress than it does about Clark's legacy.

The decision to maintain discriminatory admissions policies flowed logically from neighborhood and school segregation in Philadelphia, the commercial pressures of national television and deeply held beliefs about the dangers of racial mixing. Integrating *American Bandstand*'s studio audience in the 1950s would have been a bold move and a powerful symbol. Broadcasting daily evidence of Philadelphia's vibrant interracial teenage culture would have offered viewers images of black and white teens interacting as peers at a time when such images were extremely rare.

Clark and *American Bandstand* did not choose this path. We don't need to exaggerate the integration of *American Bandstand* to appreciate all that Clark did to shape American popular culture.

Matthew Delmont *is a professor of history at Arizona State University and the author of three books, including* The Nicest Kids: American Bandstand, Rock 'n' Roll, and the Struggle for Civil Rights in 1950s Philadelphia. *Article reprinted with permission of* Washington Post, *issue published April 22, 2012, section B2.*

Social Bandstand

Bandstand Regulars Get Together

The Regulars got together on the *American Bandstand* dance floor and at each others' houses, at parties, and at special events. Many Regulars have maintained friendships with each other for over 50 years. Here are many shots of the Regulars spending time together off the air.

FREDDY CANNON

Happy Endings

Chapter 11

Theme Parties

American Bandstand broadcast special holiday shows for Halloween, Christmas, and New Year's Eve. There were also theme shows including a swim party, a skating party, a Hong Kong party, a Roaring Twenties party, and a Western party at Frontierland.

Christmas

Skating

Roaring Twenties Party

Hong Kong Party

New Year's Eve Party

Western Party

The Oprah Winfrey Show

Dick Clark was surprised by the appearance of six Regulars during *The Oprah Winfrey Show* in 1985. The dancers featured were Arlene Sullivan, Ivette and Carmen Jimenez, Larry Giuliani, Eddie Kelly, Bobby Baritz, and Joe Ahern, who happened to also be the ABC-TV executive who discovered Oprah.

Bobby Baritz, Ivette Jimenez, and Carmen Jimenez.

Ivette, Arlene, and Carmen.

Dick Clark, Larry Giuliani, Bobby Baritz, Arlene Sullivan, Ivette Jimenez, Joe Ahern, Carmen Jimenez, and Oprah Winfrey.

Eddie Kelly, Arlene, and Carmen in the backseat, and Bobby and Larry in the front seat.

Yo! Philadelphia, Penn's Landing

Philly's Original Bandstand Dancers, 1988 to 1994

Yo! Philadelphia was the name of a three-day event that took place at Penn's Landing in Philadelphia over the Labor Day weekend. In September 1988, 20 Regulars, under the name Philly's Original Bandstand Dancers, returned to the stage for the first time since *American Bandstand* moved out to Los Angeles. From 4 p.m. to 5 p.m. before the main musical act appeared, Joe Fusco organized and led the entourage of Regulars in dancing the Slop, the Stroll, the Chalypso, and the Coffee Grinder—the original "Dirty Dancing."

Original Bandstand Dancers, 1994 to 2003

Former Regular Joanne MonteCarlo, who was working for the Philadelphia Convention Center, organized the Original Bandstand Dancers for the annual Labor Day Show. Approximately 22 dancers performed prior to the main musical act. The Original Bandstand Dancers also performed at such local events like the Thanksgiving Day Parade and the July 4th Parade. Several also went to Portugal with Mayor Ed Rendel.

American Bandstand Regulars' Alumni Association

Paul Thomas wrote to Dick Clark and Clark gave permission and his blessing to use the name *American Bandstand* Regulars' Alumni Association, for all kids who danced on the show from 1956 through 1963. About 40 Regulars joined this group and they had meetings and performed at charity events. Joanne MonteCarlo was co-president. This group lasted about 6 to 7 years.

Reunions

33 1/3 Reunion

American Bandstand Building Dedication, 1997

American Bandstand Grill Reunion, 1999

American Bandstand Grill Reunion, 2002

American Bandstand Grill Reunion, 2003

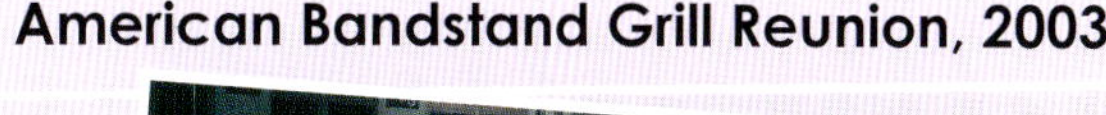

Candid Camera

American Bandstand Reunion, Sands Hotel, Atlantic City, 2005

American Bandstand, Mural Reunion, Philadelphia, 2007

Last Day in Philadelphia

The Last Day

By Pat Kinzer Mancuso

Yes, I was there on the last day of Philadelphia's *American Bandstand*: January 11, 1964. It was very emotional for me and for everybody else. We weren't happy with Dick Clark because he was moving the show to Los Angeles. The audience kept themselves busy taking pictures; I have a picture somewhere of me sitting on Bobby Baritz's lap. A bunch of us were all sitting in the back watching a playback that had just been taped.

I don't remember the guests that day, but I remember hearing "I Want to Hold Your Hand" by the Beatles for the first time. At the very end of the show, they put up the map of the US, and all of the kids danced in the middle of it; all of the Regulars were squeezing in there, trying to get on camera for the last time. Then we put on our coats and went out to the parking lot to leave. Everybody was crying and hugging.

TOP TUNES
CHANCES ARE—Johnny Mathis
LITTLE DARLIN'—Diamonds
DIANA—Paul Anka
BAND

Q & A with Sharon Sultan Cutler

Were you an *American Bandstand* fan back in the late 1950s and early 1960s?

Like many Baby Boomers, I discovered *American Bandstand* soon after it went national in mid-1957. I was ten years old, and lived in Long Island, New York. Watching the show after my afternoon snack of milk and cookies became my weekday routine before I did my homework at night.

I soon discovered I wasn't the only local kid watching Dick Clark's show because many classmates chatted about their favorite Regulars, the musical performers, and the different dances they learned. Some kids got together and watched the show while they copied the Regulars' latest dance steps. I used my basement door knob as my dance partner.

I had a huge crush on Bob Clayton, which I told him about when I interviewed him recently. We both thought that was cute.

What have you recently learned about other *American Bandstand* fans during its Philadelphia days?

Through social media and contacts with so many fans while researching this book, I realized that many fans were much more devoted to the show than I was. That helped me later during my research for the book because I had an independent, journalist's eye for details and objectivity.

During my research for the book I knew I had to set aside my own excited feelings about conversing with the Regulars. My focus was to try and elicit details about the Regulars that would make them as real today as they were to us back then.

American Bandstand gave teenage viewers a sense of belonging and respectability. Here was a program devoted to "us"—featuring neatly groomed, very attractive, and vivacious teens we could identify with.

Fans expressed their devotion to the show and the Regulars in many ways. In the Philadelphia area, hundreds of kids would line up at 46th and Market day after day, hoping to get inside the studio. Teens would also squeeze into Pop Singer's Luncheonette before and after the show, hoping to chat or take a photograph with their favorite dancers. The Regulars would often be mobbed by adoring fans when they appeared at a sock hop or local dance. Today, we might consider some fan activities as "stalking"!

Nationally, the fan clubs and the celebrity magazines fueled the public fascination with the Regulars. The popular dancers received hundreds and even thousands of fan letters weekly. As an example, Kenny Rossi became so popular he had his parents and siblings help him answer his fan mail.

The fans had amazingly strong connections and devotion to their favorite Regulars. When I looked at fan magazines from the mid-1950s on, I learned the "hot topics" might include the Regulars' favorite food, favorite color, height and weight, and even his or her home address.

How did you come up with the idea to write a book about the Regulars?

I've become more nostalgic with the memories of my tween and teenage years as I've aged. I believe that's a common denominator for many of us Baby Boomers and seniors as we look back with fondness to those simpler times when we were young at heart. We weren't burdened by adult issues and responsibilities like career,

Acknowledgments

Bandstand Diaries: The Philadelphia Years, 1956–1963 is a book that *American Bandstand* fans have waited well over 50 years to read. There were an enormous amount of helping hands involved in its creation, but we first want the Regulars who were interviewed to know that your remembrances and input are truly appreciated. We couldn't have done it without you!

Many *American Bandstand* fans wrote us, eager to share memories and photos. You generously submitted stories, old photos, fan letters, and even "xeroxes" of magazine articles from the late 1950s and early 1960s.

We send special gratitude to Al Koch, Matt Delmont, Joel Diamond, Don Gillis, Marilyn Donovan, Jean Buttz, John DeMarco, Tim Estiloz, George Yates, Patty McCann, Michael Anglemire, Ann Marie Maslan, Susan Selikson Markowitz, David Frees, Rick Fisher, Joe Marrella, Eleanor Ligman, Patricia Kinzer Mancuso, Danny Turro, Anne Marie Fusco, Sue Cassidy Wilson, Judy Willis, Sonny Maxon, Art Wilson, David Shayer, Sheryl and Sherry Davis, Homer Moyer, Stephanie Hammonds, Eileen Tanne, Cookie Horowitz Tischler, Arlene Lubman Brief (Arlene Brief Entertainment), Shelley and Michael Marks (Marks Photography), and so many more *Bandstand* admirers whose names would fill another book. We also couldn't have completed this book without the support of Vicki Cole and Lois Rosenthal.

Rock 'n' roll thanks go to Jerry Blavat, Joe Terry of Danny and the Juniors, Charlie Gracie, and Bobby Rydell for their recollections.

We thank *American Bandstand* producer Lew Klein for his memories and his photographs from those special times.

Arlene Sullivan sends a special shout of gratitude for encouragement and support to Vicki Cole, her cousins Ken and Mary Colucci, as well as her many, many friends and family members.

Ray Smith extends special thanks to: Mark Spergel, Mark Gude, Linden Chubin, Donna Case, Fran Motola, Nina Israel, Sharla Feldscher, Jim Rosin, Peggy Campbell Rowell, Lenora Hahn, B.S. Brown, Tom Furey, Sylvia Buccari, and Carole Kismaric.

Sharon Sultan Cutler wants to thank all the *Bandstand* fans who filled up her email inbox for three years with information, news, gossip, and glowing comments about the Regulars and *American Bandstand*. She wants her immediate family—Eric and Kate Goldstein, Evan and Emily Cutler, Nicole Cutler and Christine Altuna, Craig and Sandra Sultan, Judy Cutler and their children—plus her beloved extended family and friends, to know she appreciates their love and sends it right back to them. She particularly wants to thank her husband, Stephen Cutler, for his love and patience during these last three years while she was at her writing desk and on the telephone.

The *Bandstand Diaries* co-authors are so happy to have had such a wonderful production crew to make this book happen. Sharon Woodhouse, owner Conspire Creative, guided us and her team as our book's project manager. You came into our lives at the right time! We are so pleased to thank Tim Kocher, who did our retro and colorful cover design and layout; Mike Wykowski, who made a magical, vintage-looking interior design and layout, and Lydia Jones, who indexed a book filled with many difficult-to-spell names. We say "wow" and thanks again for your assistance.

Our editor, Jessica Stacy, and photographic assistant, Cameron Nass, were invaluable with their expertise. Ben Ryweck taught us the ropes of social media for our Indiegogo crowdfunding campaign, which so many friends and fans became a part of.

We give special thanks to co-author Ray Smith, whose photos of both the Regulars and the celebrities grace so many pages of this special book. Your wonderfully written chapters as well as your input throughout this entire writing and publishing process helped make this book so special.

And to Arlene Sullivan, the shy Regular who went on *American Bandstand* to get her mother's attention...well, you're still so loved and admired by fans throughout the country. Your diary proves you have another asset; you are now a bonafide author ready to go out on a book tour throughout America! Go get them, girlfriend...

Finally, thank you to the late Dick Clark, who believed before anyone else that America would embrace his little afternoon television dance party. They did—by the millions—and that revolutionized American pop culture, music, dance, and the new role teenagers played in American society in the 1950s and early 1960s. Thank you, Dick.

—Sharon Sultan Cutler

ACKNOWLEDGMENTS

The authors wish to thank the generous people who backed our 2016 Indiegogo Crowdfunding Campaign to publish *Bandstand Diaries*,

Ann d'Ercole
Albert Koch
Anita Franchetti
Ann Marie Cavaliere
Ann Marie Maslan
Annabelle Waldman
Barbara Jones
Carol Ann Hawrylak
Carol Ann Marchese
Carolyn Gilson
Carolyn Macina
Carolyn Travis
Carrolyn Hoyle Brawner
Catherine Isabella
Charlene A. Whiteside
Christine Cruickshank
Daniel K. Roberts
Diane Caraker
Don Gillis
Donna Case
Donna Reaux
Donna Vronek
Dorothy Conway
Dorothy Miley
Gabriella and Fabio Savoldelli
Fran Motola
Fran Sperling
Henry F. Burger
Helen Richardson
Irene "Bunny" Fagan
Janet Chubrick
Janet Purdy Ingram
Janet Swander
Janice Gerow
Jean Buttz
Jeremy Lamprecht
Jerry Hartley
Joel Diamond
John M. Chapman
Judy Trudgeon
Kathy Hardisty
Larry Brumbach
Lea Whitener Schlobohm
Linda Lauderdale McNabb
Linda Weiler
Linden Chubin
Lisa Burns
Luci Crittenden
Pat Kinzer Mancuso
Marilyn Donovan
Mark Gude and Paul Sekhri
Mark Spergel and Steven Catullo
Mark Tashkovich
Mary Jane Marmo
Michael Anglemire
Michael Asher
Nancy Kaufmann
Nicholas Roby
Patricia Bevacqua
Patricia Shively
Patrick Populorum
Patty Gumtow
Philippe Chambon
Ric "Kahuna" Nesbitt
Robert and Carole (Coles) Wagoner
Sharla Feldscher
Sharon Nolte
Sharon Wardlow
Sherry Davis
Sheryl Davis
Sherry Ackereizen
Skip Miller
Stanley Rifken
Steve Resinski
Susan Selikson Markowitz
Susan Wickstrom-Neville
Suzi Kaplan
Theresa LaSalle

And gratitude to the people who have reserved the Deluxe Collector's Limited Edition copy of *Bandstand Diaries*!

Amy Diaz
Angela South
Angelo Conti and Robert Zolder
Ann Marie Cavaliere
Barbara Griffin
Beverly Bosak
Bill and Gina Gabrielli
Bob and Donna Reitz
Bonnie Devine
Bud and Anne Marie Smith-Lehn
Carole Arpaia Rogers
Charles Zamal
Danny Turro
Darlene Arendt
David Frees
David and Brigette Hernandez
David and Debbie Annatone
David Myhre
Dawn and Jim Perry
Deanna (Dee) Thibodeau
Diane Iaquinto Celotto
Diane Kennedy
Dominick Alperti
Donna Druckman Fusaro
Donna Reaux
Donna Schmitt
Donna Vronek
Doris Walsh
Dorothy Bangert
Dorothy Rieger
Eileen Barone
Elsie Tillman Grady
Florence Russell
Frank and Elisabeth Levins
Glenna Gill
Gloria Phillips
Guy Elisco
Harriet Greenspan
Helen Barnes
Homer Moyer, Jr.
Jan Johnson
Janelle Macicek
Janet Burkhead
Janet Ingram
Jeanne Williams
Jeff and Kathy Sultan
Jeff Karlin
Jimmy Hudson
Joe Marrella
Joe McCahon
John Chapman
John Grayovski
John Ligos
Judith Stout
Judith Taylor
Judy Setzer
June Bouche
Karen and Robert Greenspan
Karen Ottoson
Kathleen Guzik
Kenneth O'Brien
Lee Atherton
Linda Cavallucci
Linda McNabb
Lorraine Cusato
Marcia Sherman
Margaret Chouinard
Margaret Dyess
Marie Strong
Marlyn Brown Kernan
Mary Ann Adona
Mary Ann Moore
Mary Saenz
Mary Wallace Bridges
Merle Malinowski
Mike McIntosh
Patricia McCann
Patricia Perkins
Paula Marino
Phylllis Vaquera
Rhonda Weintraub
Richard and Susan (Beltrante) Gabrielli
Rick Fisher
Ronald Forstock
Ronnie Lee
Rose Marie Rodriguez
Rosemary Pirosko
Rosemary Siermine
Ruth Gullett
Sally Ulrich
Shirley Barr-Gelfuso
Simone Braley
Sue Smith
Susan Borland Macaluso
Susan Edenzon
Sylvia Coates
Tom Williams
Wayne Weimer

Index of Names

Page numbers appearing in italic type refer to pages that contain illustrations.

G

H

I

J

K

L

About the Authors

Arlene Sullivan

Regular

Arlene Sullivan grew up in Southwest Philadelphia and was one of the most celebrated Regulars on *American Bandstand* from 1956 to 1960. Originally, Arlene went to the daily show to gain her mother's attention and approval. Fans could frequently spot her on television as she knew precisely where the cameras were. Her frequent dance partner was Kenny Rossi, who many thought was her brother because of their resemblance to each other.

After graduating from St. Monica's Commercial School in South Philadelphia, Arlene worked for Dun & Bradstreet in Philadelphia for four years. She also worked in the Warwick Hotel's sales office. When Atlantic City legalized gambling, she enrolled in a dealers' school and became a blackjack dealer. She remained in the casino business for 31 years.

Over the 55-plus years since she appeared on *American Bandstand*, Arlene has been featured in many books, as well as television, radio, and internet interviews. Her friendships with many stars include Bobby Rydell, Frankie Avalon, Fabian, Dion, and Charlie Gracie. Throughout the years, Arlene attended all of Dick Clark's Reunions and Specials, and she once appeared on *The Oprah Winfrey Show* along with some other Regulars to surprise Dick Clark.

Ray Smith

Occasional Dancer

Ray was born and raised in Philadelphia, and went to John Bartram High School along with a lot of local celebrities including: Danny and The Juniors; Patti LaBelle; Lee Andrews & The Hearts; opera singer Florence Quivar; basketball great Earl "The Pearl" Monroe; and *Bandstand* regulars, Arlene Sullivan, Peggy Leonard, and Justine Carrellli.

Ray first attended *Bandstand* in the summer of 1956. He danced on the show until Christmas 1959. In 1960, he attended Penn State as a Labor Management major. In 1964, he joined the National Guard and did basic training at Fort Jackson, South Carolina.

After working in insurance in Philadelphia, and studying acting and dance, Ray moved to New York City in 1966. He studied ballet at Richard Thomas's parents' studio, tap dance with Henry LeTang, and acting at HB Studios. He joined NBC News in 1967 and worked on the *Today Show* until he retired in 2007. He still works on the show one day a week. In 2006, he won an Emmy as part of the show's news writing team. In the late 1990s, Ray served as company manager of Noche Flamenca, the most popular and successful flamenco dance company in the world.

Ray has been a contributor to several books on rock 'n' roll. In 1997, he co-wrote *Dick Clark's American Bandstand*, and met Arlene Sullivan during an interview for the book. He and Arlene appear in Carolyn Travis's documentary *Wildwood Days*. He has a degree in film criticism from Hunter College in New York City, and worked on several films, including Bob Abel's *Let the Good Times Roll*.

Ray is most proud of his Trustees Award from Big Brothers. He is currently working on his first novel, and still taking tap and contemporary dance classes. He lives in Manhattan.

Sharon Sultan Cutler

American Bandstand *Fan*

Sharon grew up on Long Island. She watched *American Bandstand* from 1957 to 1961 on her parents' small Motorola television set, dancing remotely with the Regulars and using her basement door knob as her dance partner. She had a big crush on Bob Clayton, which she shared with him during her interview with him for *Bandstand Diaries*.

She is a journalism graduate of New York University. Over her career, Sharon has been a copywriter at Simon & Schuster, ran a Nanny–Housekeeping agency, and created Long Island's first 50-Plus Expos.

Sharon's curiosity about "whatever became of the *American Bandstand*'s Regulars" from the Philadelphia days led her to meet co-author Arlene Sullivan to discuss writing the first book about the Regulars. She went on to interview over 40 Regulars for *Bandstand Diaries*. Sharon currently lives in Chicago and visits Florida frequently.

Want More Bandstand Diaries?

Thank you to all the fans of *Bandstand Diaries* who have been amazing supporters during the research and writing of this book.

If you would like to order additional copies, please visit the online bookstore on our website at: www.BandstandDiaries.com.

If you wish to send a check to order *Bandstand Diaries*, please email us at BandstandDiaries@gmail.com, and we will send you ordering information. It is also available at Amazon.com.

To order copies in bulk for your company, organization, or book club, please write us at: BandstandDiaries@gmail.com.

To book one or more of our co-authors for an event, please contact us at: BandstandDiaires@gmail.com.

To stay in touch and join our ongoing conversations about *American Bandstand* and its Philadelphia years, follow us on Facebook (BandstandDiaries) and Twitter (@BandstandFans).